Traditional Leaded Glass Crafting

Traditional Leaded Glass Crafting

Vicki Payne

Sterling Publishing Co., Inc.
New York

Prolific Impressions Production Staff:

Editor in Chief: Mickey Baskett
Copy Editor: Phyllis Mueller
Graphics: Lampe Farley Communications
Styling: Kirsten Jones
Photography: Jerry Mucklow
Administration: Jim Baskett

Library of Congress Cataloging-in-Publication Data Available

Payne, Vicki
    Traditional leaded glass crafting : projects & techniques / by Vicki Payne
        p. m.
    ISBN 1-4027-0335-X
    1. Glass craft. I. Title.
TT298.P39 2003
748.5—dc21

2003006881

10 9 8 7 6 5 4 3 2 1

Published by Sterling Publishing Co., Inc.
387 Park Avenue South, New York, N.Y. 10016

©2003 by Prolific Impressions, Inc.

Produced by Prolific Impressions, Inc.
160 South Candler St., Decatur, GA 30030

Distributed in Canada by Sterling Publishing
c/o Canadian Manda Group, One Atlantic Avenue, Suite 105
Toronto, Ontario, Canada M6K 3E7
Distributed in Great Britain by Chrysalis Books
64 Brewery Road, London N7 9NT, England
Distributed in Australia by Capricorn Link (Australia) Pty. Ltd.
P.O. Box 704, Windsor, NSW 2756 Australia

Printed in China
All rights reserved
Sterling ISBN 1-4027-0335-X

Acknowledgements

The author wishes to thank the following companies for providing supplies used in this book:

American Bevel
www.americanbevel.com

Cascade Lead Products
1614 West 75th Ave.
Vancouver, BC V6P 6G2

Cooper Tools/Weller
P.O. Box 728
Apex, NC 27502
www.coppertools.com

Vic's Crafts
www.glasswithvickipayne.com

Glastar Corporation
www.glastar.com

Glass Accessories International
www.glassaccessories.com

Special thanks to Cindy Oppenheim, Vicki's studio assistant.

About Vicki Payne

Vicki Payne is an educational leader of the home decor and crafting industries. As CEO of Cutters Productions, she produces the nationally syndicated television shows: *Glass with Vicki Payne, Paint! Paint! Paint!, One Stroke Painting,* and *For Your Home,* which she co-hosts with her daughter, Sloan Rutter. Together, these weekly 30-minute programs are carried by more than 175 different public television stations and GoodLife TV on cable. In addition to hosting her own shows, Vicki is the host of *D.I.Y. Crafts* on HGTV's D.I.Y. Network. She is a frequent guest on home improvement and crafting shows, including *The Carol Duvall Show, Home Matters, Kitty Bartholomew: Your Home,* and *Decorating with Style.*

Vicki has produced how-to videos for over 15 years, created her own consumer glass show, *The Glass Extravaganza,* is frequently published in craft and trade magazines, and serves as a consultant to companies throughout the craft and hobby industries. She has succeeded by sharing her passion and by making her talents accessible to others.

A member of the Art Glass Association (AGA), Hobby International Association, Association of Creative Crafts, Designers Association, and the Society of Craft Designers, she has served as Chairperson of the AGA Manufacturers' Committee.

TRADITIONAL LEADED GLASS

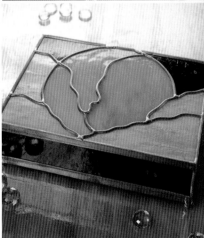

Who hasn't admired the beauty of stained glass and marveled at the rich colors, the gorgeous textures, the sparkle of the glass, the soft gleam of metal edging? But chances are you thought stained glass wasn't something you could make—it seemed so difficult, so time-consuming. Think again!

In this book, stained glass artist Vicki Payne de-mystifies the basic techniques for making leaded stained glass and presents more than two dozen leaded glass projects you can make.

First you'll learn how to choose supplies and tools. Then Vicki shows you, step-by-step, how easy it is to prepare, cut, lead up, solder, frame, and finish—everything you need to know to craft your own leaded glass projects.

You'll find instructions and patterns for making distinctive panels and window ornaments, terrific tabletop accessories like boxes and candle holders, colorful garden accessories, and ornamental birdhouses, including a bird-friendly one that's safe for feathered friends.

Relax, have fun, and enjoy the beauty of stained glass.

This framed floral panel uses the textures and grain of the various colors of glass to add interest to the design. Note the subtle color changes in the background from bottom to top.

These photos show two panels of a four-part peacock window in process. The photo at right shows the back side of the right panel, ready for soldering. The panel has been leaded up, soldered on one side, and turned so the back can be soldered.

The photo below shows the central panel in the process of being leaded up, starting in the bottom right corner.

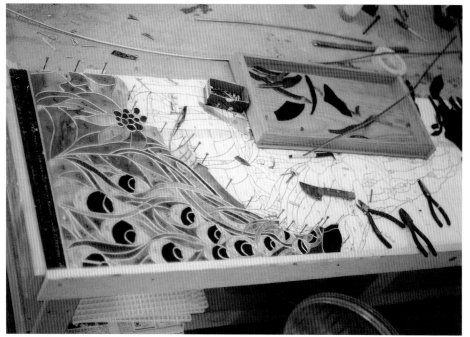

This peacock window is done with the leaded glass technique. Although it has intricate curves, the technique is still possible. Once you learn how to use the leaded glass technique, there is no limit to the designs you can create. Note how the colored glass and clear textured glass are combined in the design.

Supplies for Getting Started

Stained Glass

The terms "stained glass" and "art glass" are interchangeable—they are both used to describe types of glass manufactured for decorative purposes, as opposed to flat or float glass, which is commonly used for auto glass, windows, and doors.

There are two basic categories of stained glass: opalescent and cathedral. **Opalescent glass** is glass you cannot easily see through; **cathedral glass** is glass you can see through more clearly. Within each category there are unlimited variations and combinations of colors, textures, densities, and patterns.

Over the past few decades, the most popular type of "stained glass" isn't colored glass—it's clear art glass. Its endless variety of textures, patterns, and iridized finishes has captured my interest as an artist for over 25 years. Every time I see a new piece of glass, I can't wait to cut and shape it into my newest project.

Glass is sold by the square foot or by the pound. If you are buying glass by the square foot, you are going to get a piece of glass that is 12" x 12". If you are buying glass by the pound, you generally get 1-1/2 pounds of glass to the square foot. It is a good rule of thumb to buy about 25% more glass than the size of your project; you may use more than you anticipated. It

is always a heartbreaker to go back to the glass shop and find that there is no more of the glass you need in stock and have to wait for the next shipment to come in. Always buy more—you can save it for a future project.

You should expect to spend from $4 to $12 a square foot, depending on the color of the glass.

When choosing glass colors, the best rule of thumb is to use what you like. If you like pink, use pink. If you like yellow, select yellow. Feel free to change the colors of any of the projects in this book to suit your taste or your decor.

Rondels are handmade glass circles that have been used for centuries to fashion door and window panels. They come in a wide variety of colors and sizes. They can be used as accents or as central motifs in panels.

Flat-backed **glass nuggets** are flat on the back and rounded on the top. They come in a variety of shapes and colors and can be used as accents or as the main pieces for fanciful sculptural designs.

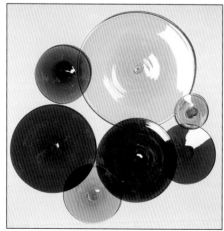

Glass rondels

Glass nuggets of various sizes. Also shown in this photo are supplies for box making: hinges, brass feet, and brass chain.

Glass Types & Textures

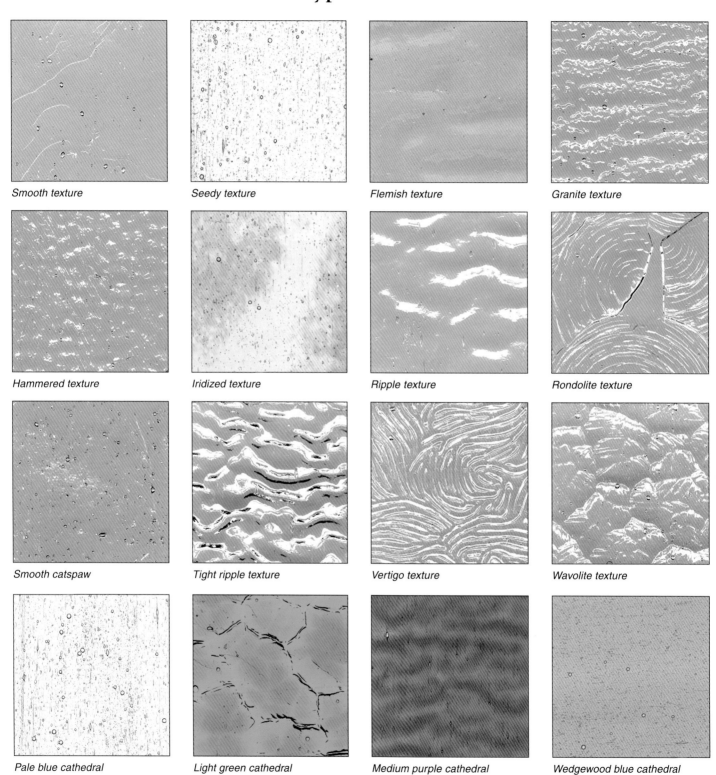

Smooth texture	Seedy texture	Flemish texture	Granite texture
Hammered texture	Iridized texture	Ripple texture	Rondolite texture
Smooth catspaw	Tight ripple texture	Vertigo texture	Wavolite texture
Pale blue cathedral	Light green cathedral	Medium purple cathedral	Wedgewood blue cathedral

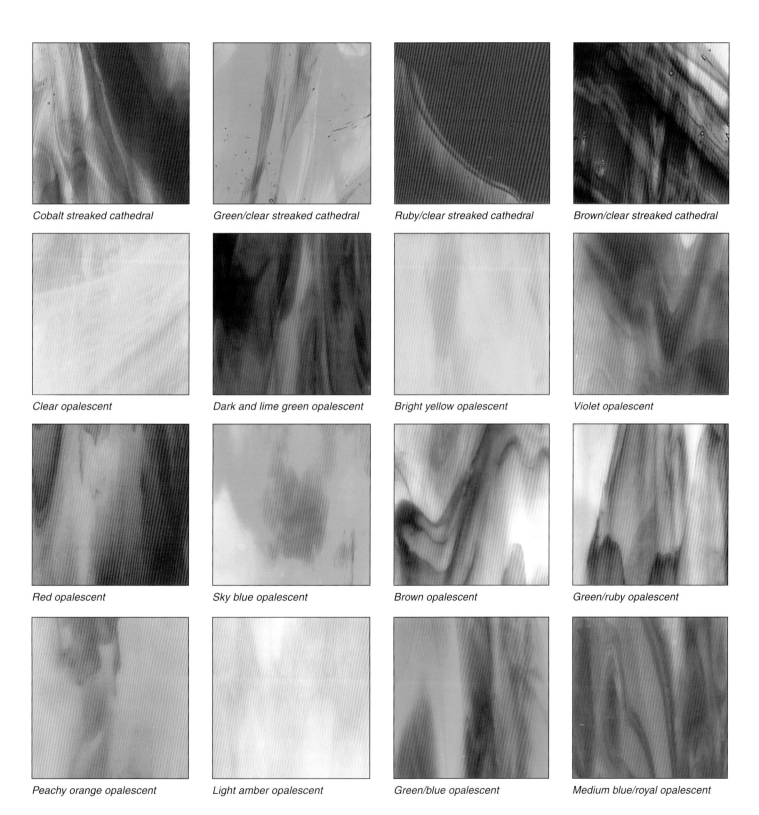

Cobalt streaked cathedral

Green/clear streaked cathedral

Ruby/clear streaked cathedral

Brown/clear streaked cathedral

Clear opalescent

Dark and lime green opalescent

Bright yellow opalescent

Violet opalescent

Red opalescent

Sky blue opalescent

Brown opalescent

Green/ruby opalescent

Peachy orange opalescent

Light amber opalescent

Green/blue opalescent

Medium blue/royal opalescent

Glass Cutting Tools

Glass cutters are the tools used to score glass so it can be cut. The score, a barely visible scratch or fissure made on the surface of the glass by the metal wheel of the cutter, weakens the glass at the site of the score and makes it easier to break.

Carbide Cutters

Handheld **carbide cutters** are the ones you'll use for most of your glass cutting. They come with different handles in a variety of styles and range in price from just a couple of dollars to about $20. The cutting wheels of all glass cutters need to be lubricated with oil, so a **self-oiling cutter** is convenient to use— it automatically lubricates the wheel as you score.

Strip Cutter

A **strip cutter** is a glass-cutting tool that can be set to a desired width. It will cut straight, parallel, uniform strips of glass again and again. It's especially useful for making boxes.

Strip-Circle Cutter

A **strip-circle cutter** is a glass cutting tool that can be set to cut both strips and circles in a range of sizes.

Lubricating Oil

Lubricating oil is necessary to protect the cutting wheel so the glass cutter will last much longer and because a score line which has been lubricated with oil is much easier to break.

If your cutter is not self-oiling, you'll need to saturate a towel with lubricating oil and keep it handy. Pass the wheel of the cutter over the oil-saturated towel before each score.

You can buy lubricating oil or mix your own. I like to use a mixture of equal amounts of motor oil and lamp oil.

Safety Gear

Protective Glasses

Always wear **protective glasses, goggles, or a face shield** when cutting and grinding glass to shield your eyes from glass chips and fragments and splattering flux or solder.

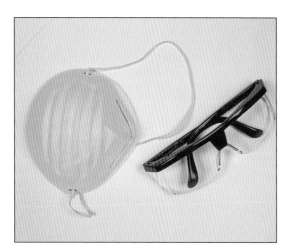

Face Mask

When you are soldering, wear a **face mask** specially designed to protect you from soldering fumes. They are available at stained glass stores and hardware stores. **Always** work in a well-ventilated area when soldering.

CAUTION!

Certain precautions should be taken when working with lead came, glass, and chemicals.

- The glass studio is not a place for small children, and older children should always be supervised when working with stained glass tools and materials.
- Lead came is toxic when mishandled. Keep your hands away from your mouth while working in lead. Make sure to wash your hands with warm water and soap before leaving your studio. If you feel like a snack, take a break. Don't eat or drink in your studio.
- Always work in a well-lighted, well-ventilated area.

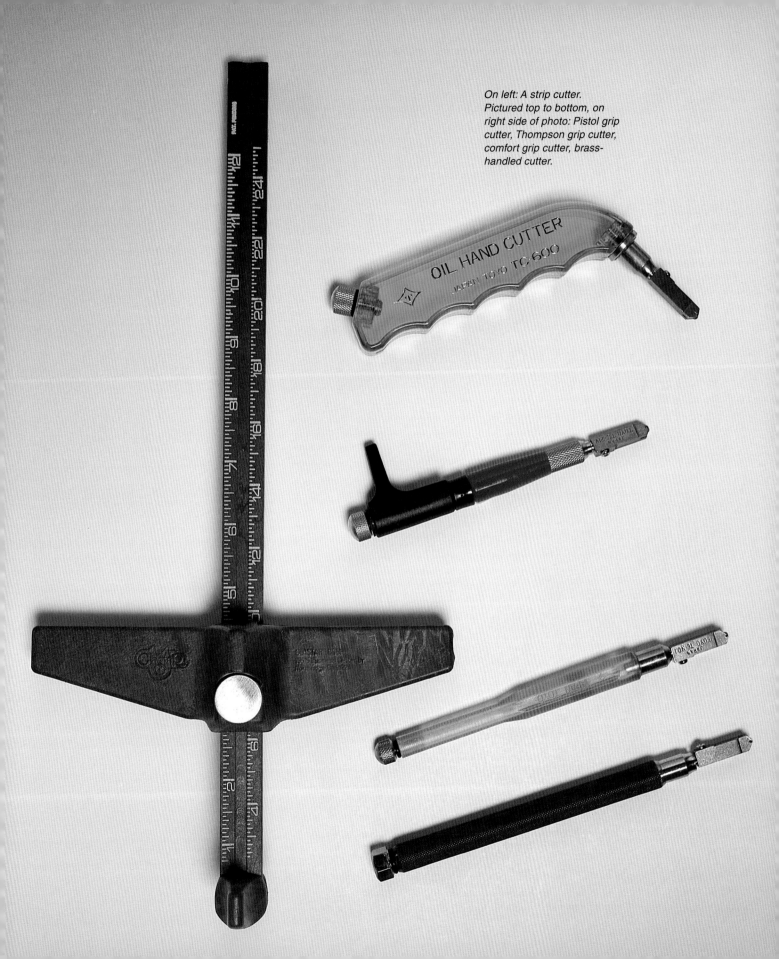

On left: A strip cutter. Pictured top to bottom, on right side of photo: Pistol grip cutter, Thompson grip cutter, comfort grip cutter, brass-handled cutter.

Glass Breaking Tools

Glass breaking tools can be used as extensions of your hands to hold and break glass.

Running Pliers

Running pliers have curved jaws with a raised ridge on the bottom and a location the ridge fits into on the top. Use running pliers to help you push the score line through the glass so you can break it with the pliers instead of with your hands. The mark on the top jaw helps you position the pliers on the score line.

Breaking Pliers

Breaking pliers have jaws that are flat on the inside. When you need to hold a piece of glass to break it and do not have room for two hands, use these.

Grozing Pliers

Grozing pliers have little teeth like a file on both the top and the bottom jaws. Use these pliers to chip away at the little unwanted pieces of glass that remain along a cut after scoring and breaking.

Combination Pliers

Combination pliers have a flat jaw and a curved jaw. Both jaws are serrated. Combination pliers can be used both for breaking and grozing. Use the curved side up for grozing and the flat side up for breaking.

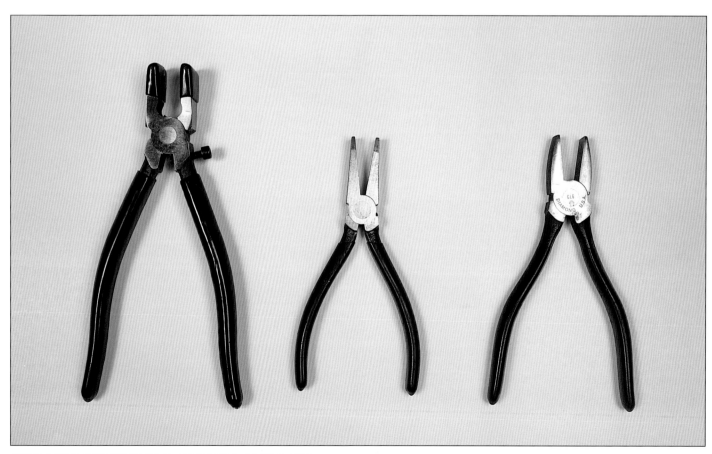

Pictured left to right: running pliers, grozing pliers, breaking pliers.

Glass Smoothing Supplies

Glass smoothing supplies prepare the edges of cut glass pieces for the leading technique and correct minor problems in the shape of a piece of glass, ensuring that pieces will fit together as intended.

Glass Grinder

An electric **glass grinder** is a machine with a diamond bit and a tray underneath the bit that contains water. There is a sponge in the back that pumps water up to the bit to keep it wet when you are grinding. The water keeps the dust down and keeps the glass cool so it will not fracture.

A grinder is the fastest, most efficient way to prepare and correct problems on the edges of glass pieces, but grinders are not inexpensive. You might want to check with your local glass shop about renting one. When you use a glass grinder, **always** wear safety glasses and follow the manufacturer's instructions.

Emery Cloth/Carborundum Stone

An **emery cloth** or a **carborundum stone** also may be used to smooth the edges of cut glass pieces. Be forewarned that using the carborundum stone or emery cloth is a slow process, but less expensive than buying a grinder.

Pictured top to bottom: Carborundum stone, emery cloth.

A glass grinder.

Pattern Making Supplies

When you are first starting out, it is better to use a pattern designed specifically for stained glass. When you become more experienced, you can create your own designs. Use these supplies to make patterns for cutting out glass pieces and assembling your projects.

Pattern Paper

I like to use **white bond paper or white craft paper** for patterns—white instead of brown because it is easier to see the colors of the colored pencils. If you use a light box for tracing the pattern lines on the glass, white paper is easier to see through.

Tracing Paper

Use **tracing paper** and a **pencil** to trace patterns from this (and other) books. Buy tracing paper at crafts and art supply stores.

Transfer Paper

Use **transfer paper** to transfer designs to pattern paper. You can also use a photocopier to make copies of traced designs.

Colored Pencils

Cutting the pieces for your stained glass projects is easier if you take the time to color in the design with **colored pencils**. That way, you create a color-keyed pattern that's especially helpful when you cut the pattern up to make templates for cutting the glass.

Pictured clockwise from left: Pattern paper, tracing paper, pattern shears, pencil, masking tape, rubber cement, transfer paper, ruler.

Ruler

The most important tool you need is a **metal ruler**. An 18" ruler is a good size to have. Make sure it's calibrated from one end all the way to the other. Also make sure it has a cork back. This will prevent it from slipping around while you are drawing and using it to cut glass.

Pattern Shears

Stained glass is composed of pieces of glass separated by pieces of metal all the way across a project, and the metal takes up space between each piece of glass. When you cut out pattern pieces with **pattern shears** to make templates for cutting your glass, the special blades of the pattern shears (there are three of them) remove a small strip of paper on the cutting lines to allow space for the metal.

You might want to practice cutting with pattern shears on some scrap paper before you cut out your pattern to make templates.

Rubber Cement

Use **rubber cement** or a **pattern fixative** to hold pattern pieces in place for cutting and grinding. Either will simply rub off the glass when you're ready to construct your piece.

Masking Tape

You also need **masking tape** to hold your design in place on your work board and for holding together pieces of glass for birdhouses, lampshades, and boxes together until you solder them.

Markers

To mark on glass, choose markers that aren't permanent on glass and can be rubbed or washed off. Test **felt-tip markers** on a scrap of glass before using. A **china marker**, available at crafts and art supply stores in a variety of colors, is another good choice for marking glass.

Other Supplies

It is a good idea to get a **shoebox** to put your cut-apart pattern pieces in so you don't lose any of them. If you do happen to lose a pattern piece during the process of building your window, you can always make a tracing off your other (un-cut) copy.

Pattern shears have three cutting blades.

Came

There are two techniques used to create stained glass projects: the copper foil technique and the leaded glass technique. This book will teach the LEADED GLASS TECHNIQUE which is the more traditional method. This technique connects individual pieces of glass by fitting them into metal channels called cames.

Came comes in a variety of sizes and metal types; the most common is lead, but you will also find came made from hard metals such as zinc, brass, or copper. The places cames meet or intersect within a project are called joints. The joints are soldered to create a strong, continuous metal frame around each individual glass piece within the project.

There are two basic came shapes:

- **H-shaped cames** are used in the interior portions of a project because they are designed to accept glass from two sides.

- **U-shaped cames** are used to wrap the exterior perimeter of a panel or an individual piece of glass when constructing a box, candle cube, or birdhouse.

Came is sold in 6 ft. strips in various sizes. The size is determined by the width of the came face. The face can be flat, round, or colonial. The channel height is generally 3/16" high, but you can special order what are called "high heart" cames, which have a bigger channel, for projects such as pressing flow-

Various types of came.

22

ers between two pieces of glass.

Select your came size based on the size of the glass pieces and the intricacy of the design. The smaller the came face, the less support it provides large glass pieces; the larger the face, the bulkier the look. If you are building a front door panel with bevels, you would want 3/8" or 3/16" came. But for a floral window with lots of small pieces, you would use 1/16" or 1/8" came. Lead, unlike foil, gives you a smooth flowing lead line that highlights the design, not the metal.

The decision to work with lead came or one of the hard metal came types depends on the size of the project, where the project will be installed, and how many curves are in the design. Lead is very flexible, easy to work with, and can easily be cut and trimmed to shape using lead nippers or a lead knife.

Hard metal cames extruded from brass, zinc, or copper provide maximum strength but can be more difficult to work with, especially if your project contains

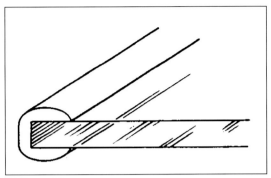

U-Shaped Came.

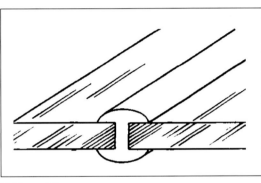

H-Shaped Came.

curved lines and angles. Some gentle shapes and curves can be done by hand, but others require the use of a came bender. Hard metal cames must be cut with a hacksaw or power came saw. If you are going to work with hard metal came, do yourself the favor of investing in a good came saw and a came bender. They will provide you years of unlimited design and project possibilities.

Cames are also selected because of their colors. Brass cames are elegant, and brass provides excellent strength and lasting beauty. Zinc cames are silver, and they work very well in contemporary panels or when sparkle of both glass and metals is desired. Copper came is perfect for southwestern-style panels or when matching copper or Arts & Crafts hardware or decor. All solder joints are silver but can be treated with a patina or painted to match any color of came.

Whether you work with lead or hard metal came, the process of assembling your panel or project is called "**leading up.**"

Leading Tools

Most of the lead came you will use to "lead up" small to medium projects is very soft and can easily be cut and bent with hand tools. Following is a description of some of the hand tools that will be necessary when working with lead came. If you are working on large window panels that need to be very stable, you may need to work with hard metal came which would require powers saws.

Pictured left to right: Lead knife with sharpening stone, lead nippers, fid (lathekin)

Leading Knife

A leading knife primarily is used to cut lead cames into various lengths. The blade needs to be sharpened regularly on a whetstone or sharpening stone to keep from crushing the heart of the came when cutting. The end of the handle has a lead inlay, which is used to gently tap glass pieces into the came channels and to hammer horseshoe nails into your work board when leading up a project.

Lead Nippers

A quick and easy way to trim lead came is with nippers. Nippers are best for cutting straight cuts or slight angles. For more long, tapered cuts a lead knife works best. You will want to learn how to use both tools.

Fid (Lathekin)

Opening crushed or tight came channels is easier with a lathekin, which is also called a fid.

Using a fid to open the channel in a piece of lead came.

Lead Vise

All lead cames must be stretched before you use them. Stretching takes out any small kinks and adds strength. A lead vise holds one end of the came while you hold the opposite end with a pair of household pliers and gently pull or stretch the came.

Inserting one end of a strip of lead came in a lead vise.

Came Notcher

A came notcher is used to cut 1/8" U-shaped hard metal came at a 45-degree angle without cutting through the back spine of the came, giving you perfectly mitered corners for framing projects or wrapping individual glass pieces.

If you do not have a notcher, you can cut U-shaped cames with wire cutters or nippers.

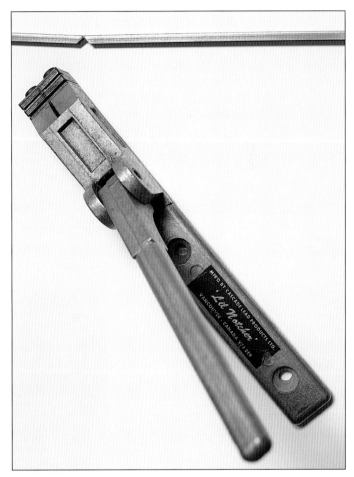

A came notcher.

Came Saw

A came saw is a small power chop saw that uses a fiber or metal circular blade to cut hard metal cames. It is a must if you are going to build large panels with hard metal came.

A came saw is used to cut hard metal came.

Came Bender

Hard metal cames benefit greatly from being bent with a came bender. The device bends the came without scarring the came face or crushing the channel. The bender's rotating wheels can be adjusted to conform to almost any shape. Came benders can be permanently attached to your work table or held securely with a c-clamp.

Bending hard metal came in a came bender.

Soldering Tools & Supplies

*After all the glass pieces are in place and leaded up with came, then the joints
of the came have to be soldered. You will need the following supplies.*

Flux and Brush

Flux is a cleaner that prepares metal to accept the solder. Without flux, soldering isn't possible. I recommend a water-soluble flux, which can be washed off your project with dish-washing soap and water and can be left on your project overnight or until the next day without doing damage.

When you're working, it's a good idea to pour some flux out of the container it comes in and into a wide-mouth jar. Don't ever go back and forth from the container the flux comes in to your project. You'll weaken the strength of the flux if you do.

Apply flux to your project with a **flux brush**. These brushes rust out after a while (continuing exposure to the flux corrodes them), so it's a good idea to buy a couple at a time.

Solder

Solder is the molten metal used to join the metal-wrapped glass pieces. It looks like thick wire and comes on a spool. When doing the leaded glass technique, you'll work with a solid-core solder labeled "50/50." The numbers indicate what percentage tin (50%) and lead (50%) are in the solder.

continued on page 28

Pictured from top left: Soldering iron rheostat with iron holder, 80 watt soldering iron, flux and flux brush, solder, 100 watt thermostatically controlled soldering iron.

Soldering Tools
continued from page 27

Soldering Iron with Rheostat

To solder stained glass, you need a **soldering iron**, not a soldering gun. You can't use a soldering gun on your stained glass project. The **rheostat** controls the temperature of the soldering iron. Soldering irons have tips of various sizes that come with them. For most projects, a tip 1/4" wide is used.

An **iron stand** keeps your iron from rolling around on your work surface and protects you from the hot parts of the iron when you are working.

Tip Cleaner

A **tip cleaner** is simply a sponge that is kept wet so that you can wipe off the tip of your soldering iron as you work to keep it clean and completely shiny. If you work with a soldering iron tip that is all dark, you won't be able to do a good job of soldering.

Assembly Supplies

Glass Squaring Bars

These bars are used along the outer perimeter of a panel to help you square up your project after it is built. You can make your own squaring bars by cutting various lengths of clear glass into 1-1/2" strips. You will need bars from 12" to 24" in length. Wrap the edges in masking tape.

Horseshoe Nails

Horseshoe nails have two flat sides and a large square head. They are used to hold pieces of glass in the

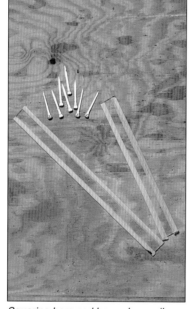

Squaring bars and horseshoe nails

channels while the panel is being leaded up. They hammer into a wooden work board easily and can be pulled free with just a gentle wiggle. Horseshoe nails bend easy. When they do, throw them away. Trying to work with a bent nail isn't worth the hassle.

Lead Spacers

Damaged or scrap pieces of lead came (the same type and size used for your project) are needed to temporarily space the glass pieces during assembly.

Work Space

It is important to select a work table that is at a comfortable height with enough space to accommodate your project when it is completely built plus all the tools and supplies you need to build the project. In your work space, you also want to make sure you have good lighting, convenient access to electrical outlets, good ventilation, and a hard-surface floor that is easy to clean.

Work Boards

Your work board is the surface you'll use for assembling your glass projects. It should fit comfortably on your work table and be at least 2" bigger than the project you're making. A **plywood work board** is best for leading up panels. I like to use 3/8" or 1/2" thick plywood.

You'll need to form a right angle on two sides of your work board for leading up panels. I like to use 1" x 1" stop molding for this. Use a **carpenter's triangle** or **framing square** and double check the angle you construct (more than once!) to make sure it's perfectly square. If you don't start out square, you will never be able to build a square project!

For copper foil work, another option is to make your work board from **Homasote**, a building material that's often used to make bulletin boards. Buy plywood and Homasote at building supply stores.

If your work space is limited, you can make a portable work board and store it behind a door or in the garage. Don't paint or varnish your work boards; the heat of the soldering process will cause the lead came to stick to the finish.

Crafting Your First Lead Came Project

Stained glass is a beautiful puzzle that's easy to construct one step at a time—a piece of lead, a piece of glass, a piece of lead, a piece of glass until the panel is completed. In this section, you'll see how to cut out a pattern, cut glass, use a grinder, lead up the panel, solder, and frame the finished project for display.

How Much Glass?

For the projects in this book, the amount of glass you need to complete the project is included in the Supplies list for each project. I wanted to make that part easy because estimating how much glass you need can cause problems for even experienced glass workers. Here are some guidelines, using the Art Nouveau Tulip Panel project that follows as an example.

For the background of the panel, which measures 12" x 8", if you bought a 12" x 12" piece of glass, you would have enough glass to cut out all of the pieces and, if necessary, enough to re-cut a couple of the pieces if you have a problem. To cut out the flower and the leaves, you are going to need about twice as much glass as the space you are filling on the panel. It would be a good idea to get twice as much pink glass as the area of the flower to give enough space to rotate the pattern pieces so the grain of the glass is going in the most attractive direction.

For this first project, the background is cream opalescent glass, and you need to buy one square foot. For the pink tulip, you need to buy one-half square foot. For the green opalescent leaves, you need another one-half square foot.

Art Nouveau
Tulip Panel

The project used as an example is a beautiful framed panel with a tulip design. It's a wonderful place to start because it requires only three colors of glass. The pattern allows you to experience a variety of cuts. All of the pieces in this book use the same techniques for cutting and assembly.

Size: 11" x 16"

Supplies

Glass:
2 sq. ft. light green cathedral
6" x 6" piece red cathedral
6" x 6" piece dark green cathedral
7" x 3" dark purple cathedral

Came:
2 6-ft. strips of 3/16" H lead
1 6-ft. strip of 3/8" H lead (for perimeter)

Other Supplies:
Cementing supplies (see page 53)

Tools:
Basic Tools & Supplies

Step 1 • Prepare Your Pattern

Pattern is on page 56

When creating a pattern for a lead came project you must take into consideration the space taken up by the lead heart and outside edges of the came.

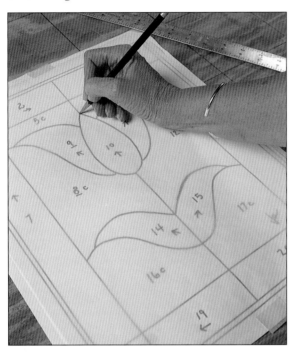

1. Position tracing paper over the pattern and trace the design lines with a pencil.

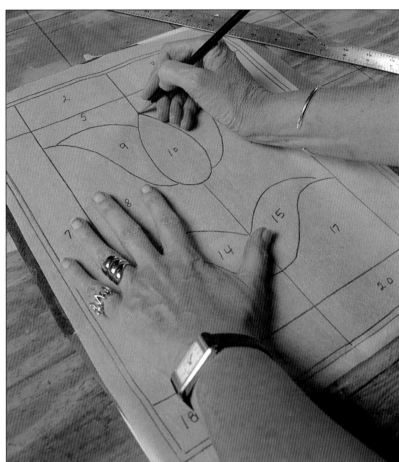

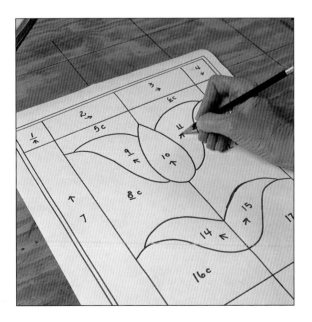

2. Transfer the design to white pattern paper or photocopy the traced design and enlarge as noted. You want to have two copies of the pattern—one to cut apart to make templates for cutting the glass and another to use as a guide when assembling the piece.

3. Use arrows to mark the desired direction of the grain of the glass on your two working copies of the pattern (the one you will cut apart and the one you will use for assembling). Number the pattern pieces. *Option:* Color-code the pattern with colored pencils that correspond with glass colors you've chosen. This makes it easier to identify the pattern pieces after you've cut them apart for the cutting templates.

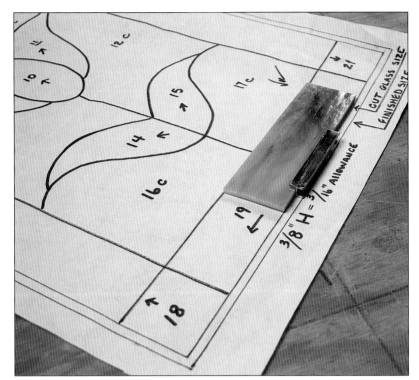

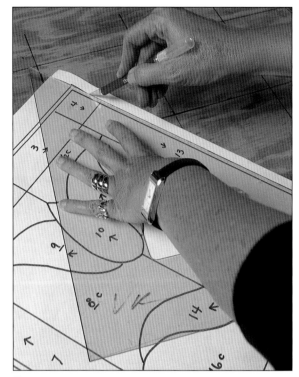

4. The two patterns are ready to have their edges trimmed. The "finished size" is the size your project will be once it is completed. The "cut size" is the size you will cut your glass pieces. The cut size dimensions take into account the came heart and outside channel of the lead (so the panel will end up the "finished size"). The "sight size" of a piece is the area you actually see after the glass is inserted in the came channel.

5. Using a craft knife, cut out one pattern for assembling the panel on the "finished size" lines. Use a ruler or a triangle to get a clean, straight edge.

6. Use the second traced pattern for making templates. Cut off the outer edges of the pattern on the "cut size" lines. Use a ruler or triangle and a craft knife to get a clean, straight edge.

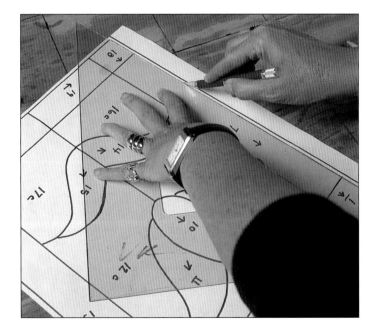

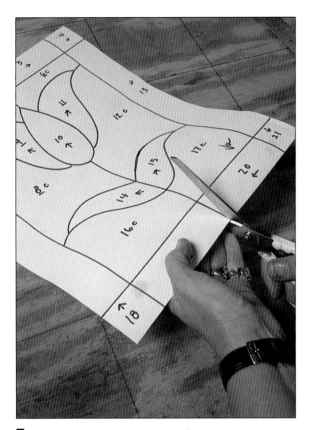

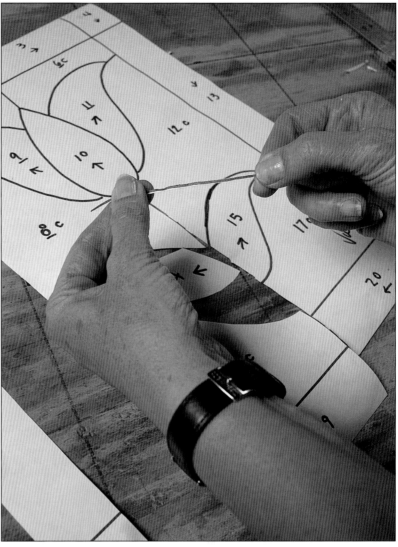

7. Use pattern shears to cut out the pattern pieces you will use as cutting templates. Put the single blade up toward you and start cutting with small strokes, not big sweeping ones. Hold the pattern in your other hand and cut right along the line, cutting in the crux of the shears. Continue cutting until you have cut out every piece of your pattern. The order you cut it out doesn't matter; do whatever seems easiest for you.

8. The three blades of the pattern shears work together to remove a strip of paper that accommodates the space needed for the came heart.

Step 2 • Cut the Glass Pieces

Caution! Always wear safety glasses to protect your eyes when cutting glass.

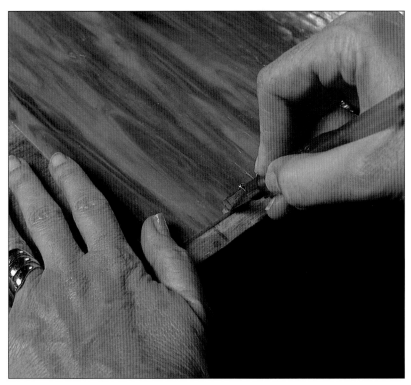

1. Determine how much glass you will need to cut your first piece by positioning the pattern piece on the glass. Score a smaller, more manageable piece of glass from the large glass sheet using your glass cutter. (You'll cut out the pattern piece—in this case, it's a leaf—from the smaller piece of glass.) Begin scoring, positioning your glass cutter at the edge of the large piece. Pull cutter down length of glass.

2. To break the glass, pick it up and put your fingers on each side of the scored line, under the glass, with your thumbs on top. Rock your hands up and away from you. The glass will break along the scored line.

3. Apply pattern fixative or rubber cement to backs of pattern pieces. There is a right side and a wrong side to glass for cutting. The right side—the front—is generally smoother. The wrong side—the back—has a little bit of a bump to it. Position the pattern pieces on the right (smooth) side of glass, aligning the arrows you marked on the pattern pieces with the grain of the glass. Allow 1/4-1/2" all around each piece to make breaking out the pieces easier. Cut the larger piece into two smaller pieces, scoring a line between the pattern pieces. Break the glass.

Option: If you have a light box, you can place the pattern on the light box and position the glass over the pattern. (The pattern lines will be visible through the glass.) Use a china marker or felt-tip marker (one that's not permanent on glass) to transfer the pattern lines to the glass.

4. To begin cutting the first pattern piece, start the cut at the edge of the piece of glass and move the cutter along the edge of the pattern template. Finish the cut by continuing past the edge of the pattern template and off the edge of the glass. This photo shows scoring the inside curve.

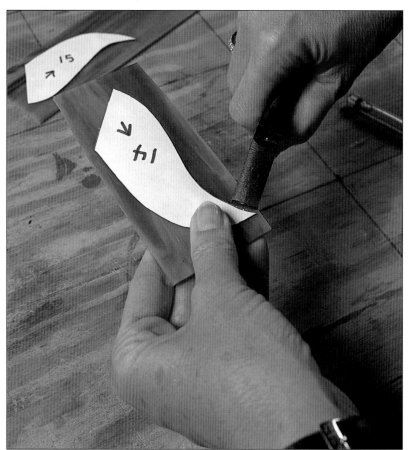

5. Break the glass with breaking pliers. Hold the glass off the work surface in one hand and hold the pliers in your other hand. Position the edge of the pliers on the scored line. Breaking pliers work well on curved cuts.

6. Use the same technique to score and break the outside curve.

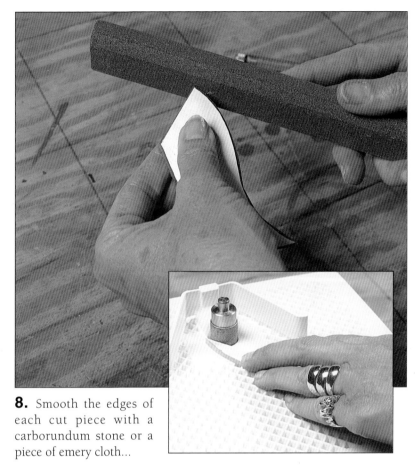

7. Use grozing pliers to break away any small chips or flanges of glass that protrude on the edges of cut pieces. You will save a lot of time if you use your grozing pliers to remove most of the unwanted glass before you use the grinder or smoothing stone. **TIP:** To ensure a clean work surface, periodically sweep off your work surface with a brush to remove small chips and slivers of glass that accumulate as you work.

8. Smooth the edges of each cut piece with a carborundum stone or a piece of emery cloth...

Or use an electric glass grinder to smooth the edges. Keep the pattern pieces attached to the glass as you work on the edges.

9. To cut deep curves, make successive scores and breaks to gradually move into the final cut. The dotted lines show how this background piece could be scored and separated.

10. Use running pliers to break the glass on straight cuts, like this border piece. Score the glass from one edge to the other along the pattern template's edge. Align the mark on the running pliers with the scored line.

11. Squeeze the pliers to break the glass.

Step 3 • Preparing & Cutting Lead Came

1. Lead cames must be stretched before you use them. **Never** stretch came until you are ready to lead up your panel—and then **only** stretch the came you will be using that day. To estimate how much you will need, use a tape measure to measure the leading lines in your pattern. Add the measurements together and add 25% of that number to the total.

Once came is stretched, it starts to oxidize. The oxidation process tarnishes the came and makes it more difficult to solder if left for a period of time. The first step in stretching the came is to insert one end of the piece in a lead vise.

2. Hold the other end of the came with a pair of pliers and pull. The stretching process requires a little experience to know when you have stretched the lead just the right amount. Generally speaking, you want to stretch a 6-ft. piece of came 3-4". Overstretching the came will stress the lead, making it stiffer, and will narrow the channel height, making it more difficult to insert glass in the channel. Once your came is stretched, remove it from the vise. Use your lead nippers to trim 2" off each end of the came, and discard the lead scraps.

3. Using your lead nippers, cut six to ten 2" strips of came to be used as spacers while leading up the panel. If you are working with two or more sizes of came, cut additional spacers from each size. Have lots of horseshoe nails on hand and a pointed felt-tip marker.

4. The leading knife is a valuable tool that must be kept sharp for cutting to avoid crushing the came. To make sure your lead knife is nice and sharp, sharpen it regularly on a sharpening stone.

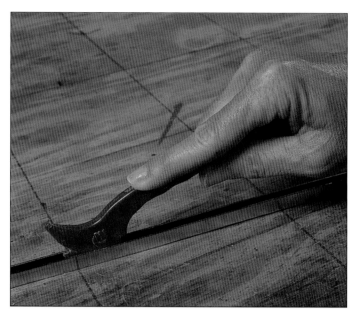

5. Draw a lathekin (fid) down the lead came channel on one side; then turn the strip over and repeat on the other side. This removes dents (small or large) and opens up the channel so the glass will fit in it easily.

6. To cut came, place the came on a firm wooden surface, channel side up. Place the sharpened lead knife blade on the lead.

7. Gently push down with the knife while rocking it side to side until it cuts through the channel and heart.

9. Angles can also be cut with lead nippers. Mark the angle on the came; then use the nippers to make a straight cut.

8. To cut angles with the knife, place the came channel side up and place the blade at a 45 degree angle. Use that same rocking motion to cut a longer miter.

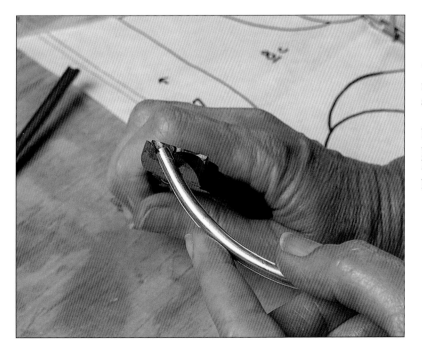

10. Line up the nippers with the mark on the came and cut the angle.

Note: Don't bother saving leftover pieces of lead. Check with your local recycling facility about disposal of discarded lead scraps.

Step 4 • Assemble the Project

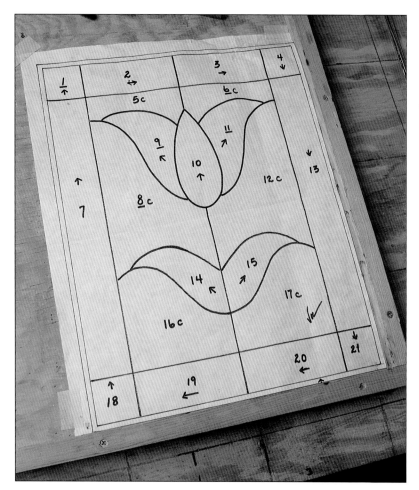

2. Cut two pieces of perimeter came the same length as the panel you are building. Place them on top of your pattern alongside the wooden stop molding.

1. Use your second copy of the pattern as a guide for leading up your project. Start by using a craft knife and ruler to trim off two edges of the pattern at the "finished size" line to form a trimmed right angle that can be positioned in the corner of your work board. (You will learn with experience that it is often easier to lead up a panel if you start in one corner.) Use masking tape to secure your pattern to the work board.

Lay out all your glass pieces in numerical order or, if space allows, lay them out in the mirror image of the design. You will remove the pattern pieces from the glass as you use each piece but for now leave the patterns attached.

3. Secure the ends of the came pieces with horseshoe nails.

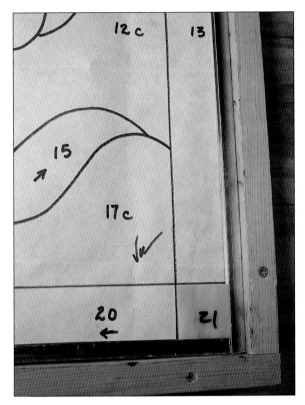

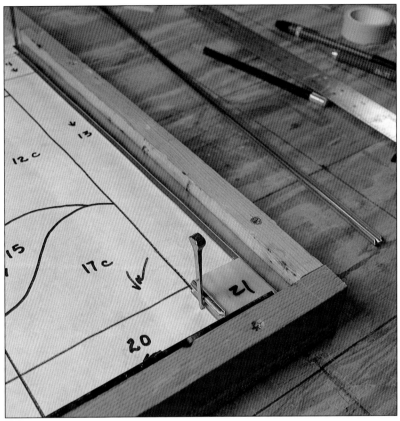

4. Matching the numbers on the pattern to the numbers on the glass pieces, select the first corner piece. Remove the pattern paper from the piece and slip the glass in the lead came channels. Check around the outside edges of the glass piece. Make sure you can see the pattern line around all the exposed edges. If not, mark the area with your felt-tip marker and remove the piece. Use the glass grinder or grozing pliers to remove the excess glass. Continue putting in and checking the piece until it fits perfectly!

The secret to successfully building lead came windows is to stay on pattern. If you're ever tempted to tell yourself "maybe this won't be a problem," resist! Stop, take out the piece, and fix it. This goes for a piece that's too small as well as for one that's too large. If there is too much space between the edge of the glass piece and the pattern line, the glass piece may not stay in the channel.

5. Once you are happy with the fit, use a discarded piece of came as a lead spacer to "face the glass"—simply slip the spacer on the outside edge of the glass piece and secure with a horseshoe nail. **Never** put a nail directly against the edge of the glass or against a good piece of came (one you're using to build your project). The nail will chip the glass and mar the face of the came.

6. Fit a good piece of lead came on the edge of the glass and mark for cutting. This photo shows marking the lead by denting it with a leading knife.

8. Place the lead against the glass piece.

7. Cut the length of lead came to fit against glass piece as you have marked. Use lead nippers to cut lead.

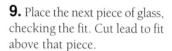

9. Place the next piece of glass, checking the fit. Cut lead to fit above that piece.

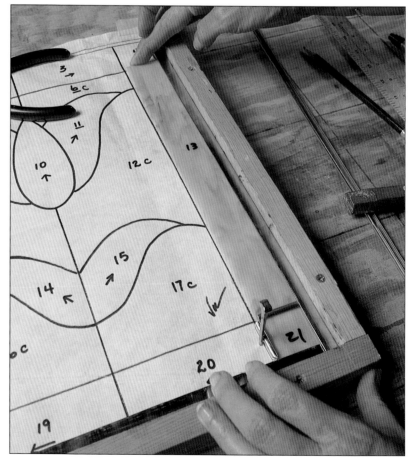

10. Continue to add pieces of glass and pieces of lead came, working up the right side. Cut and fit a piece of lead along the left side of all three glass pieces. Add the piece of glass along the bottom, then the first interior piece.

11. Curved pieces are easy to lead because the lead is very pliable. Cut off a section of came that's large enough to wrap along the outside edge of the glass piece. Position the came over the top of the glass edge and gently mold the came with your hands to mirror the angle of the glass piece.

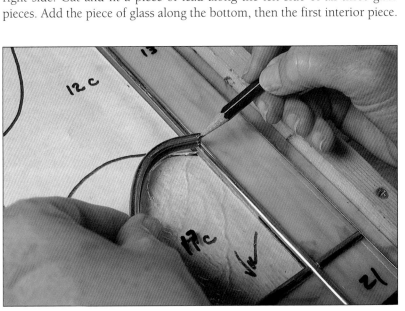

12. Mark the angles of the cuts. This photo shows marking the lead with a pencil. You can use a pencil to mark where to cut the lead or dent it with a knife to indicate cutting line.

13. Trim the lead to size.

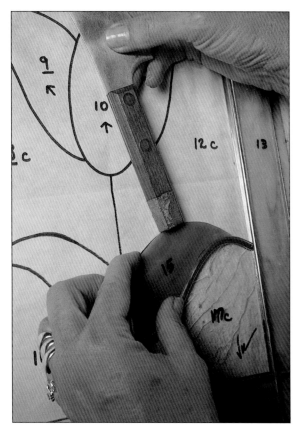

14. Remove the nail and spacer lead and slip the trimmed came in place. Push the came up on the glass edge and continue to mold the lead to fit the glass. *Tip:* Use the end of your fid to get a nice snug fit. Secure this lead came in place using another lead spacer and a nail. This is called "facing the came."

15. Working out from the corner, select the next piece of glass to lead up. If the piece doesn't slip into the channel easily, place the piece and tap gently on the edge with the handle of your knife to secure. (Don't be worried about selecting the wrong piece—you will quickly learn which piece to use next. The worst thing that can happen is that you will need to remove it and try another piece.)

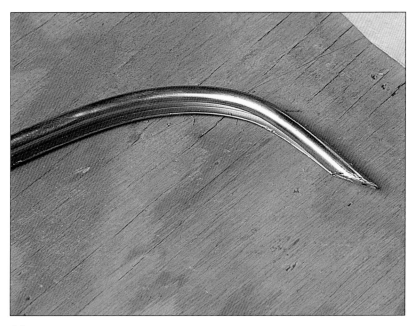

16. When the lead pieces intersect with other pieces of came, they may need to be cut at an angle to ensure proper fit.

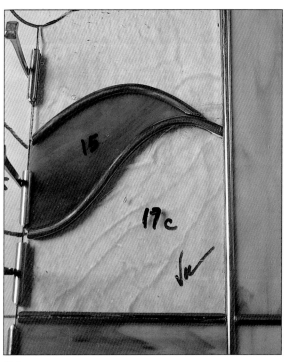

17. Place the lead around the leaf. Note how the angled cut makes a smooth flowing line of lead.

18. Continue placing and fitting glass pieces. If a piece of glass is too big (as this one is, extending over the pattern line), mark the correct size with a felt tip marker.

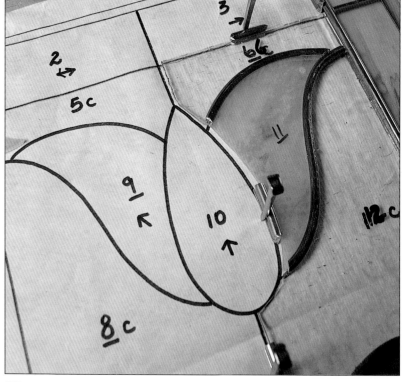

19. Use grozing pliers to remove some glass from the edge so pieces will fit better.

20. Replace the glass and check the fit. This time, it's correct.

21. The center petal of the tulip is wrapped with a piece of came. First, cut a piece of came long enough to fit around the piece and cut a 45-degree angle on one end. Wrap the piece, making sure the glass is secure in the channel. *Tip:* It's better to have a piece of came that's a little too long. You can always trim off, but you can't add.

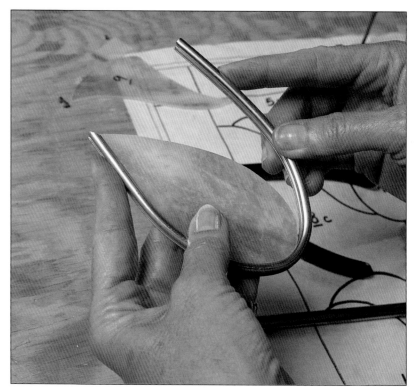

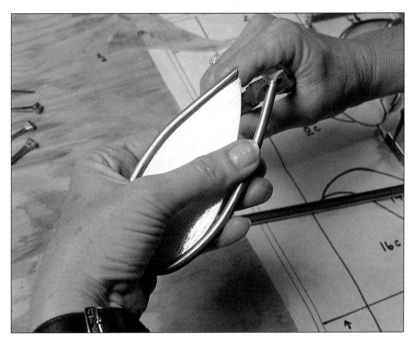

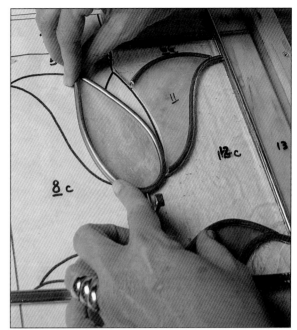

22. Where the ends meet, mark the other end and cut the came at an angle for a smooth fit.

23. The lead-wrapped piece is pressed into place.

24. The right half of the panel is leaded up.

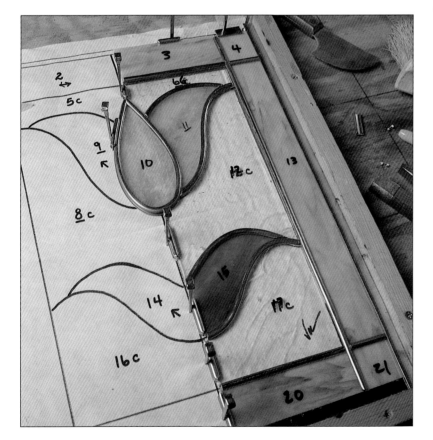

25. The left side of the panel, which is a mirror image of the right, is leaded up and ready for the lead on the edge. Take care to run the lead on the second half of the panel the same way you did on the first.

26. Once all the pieces are leaded up, you are ready to add the two remaining perimeter came pieces. This is called "capping off." Place the pieces of came on the top and left side. To make sure the edge pieces are secure, slip a squaring bar the length of the panel in the outside lead channel (or against the back of the lead, if the panel is framed in U-shaped came). Check to make sure you can still see your "finished size" pattern line around the edges of the came. If not, use the lead inlay in the handle of your lead knife to gently tap along the edge of the squaring bars. This will evenly shift all the glass pieces at once and allow you to snug up your design and correct minor out-of-square problems.

27. The panel is ready for soldering.

Step 5 • Solder the Panel

To solder lead came, use 50/50 solder and a soldering iron and rheostat combination or a thermostatically controlled iron of 80 to 100 watts.

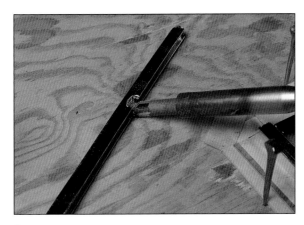

1. Test the temperature by holding the soldering iron tip on a scrap piece of lead came. If it melts the lead, it is too hot. Turn the iron down and re-test in a few minutes. You want your iron hot enough to quickly turn solder into a flowing liquid but not so hot that it melts the lead came.

Soldering Tips

- Always use a soldering iron stand to secure your iron.
- If you need to re-heat a solder joint to touch up or lower a tall solder joint, always re-flux first.
- Solder will not stick to glass, but avoid touching the tip of your hot soldering iron to the glass surface.

Soldering Hard Metals

Soldering hard metals is a little different. You can use more heat because the metals don't melt as quickly. Hard metals require less solder because they are not as porous. Because hard metals heat much more quickly than lead, never try to hold a piece of hard metal in place with your fingers while soldering.

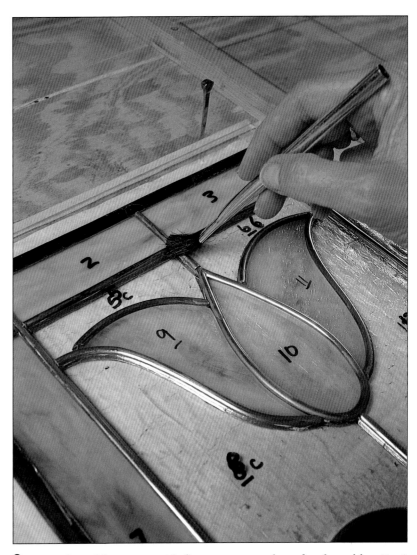

2. Paint the solder joints with flux to prepare them for the solder. Don't worry about being exact with the flux.

3. Place the end of the solder wire over the joint and apply heat, using the flat side of the iron. Hold in place until the solder flows smooth and flat over the joint. Use just enough solder to hide the lead's intersection but not so much that there's a ridge or a "button."

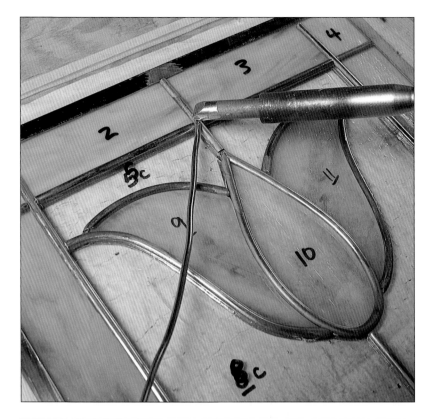

4. Keep solder joints small and flat around the perimeter of the panel so it will be easier to frame or install. When you complete one side, turn the panel over and solder the back side.

Step 6 • Cementing

Cementing is done to make a project more stable and durable. It is an optional procedure. All came panels such as windows or framed pieces should be cemented. It is not necessary to cement small projects. Cementing makes the panel airtight and waterproof and keeps the glass from rattling inside the came channels. You can mix up cement using my formula (the recipe follows) or use pre-mixed cement. (Pre-mixed leaded glass cement is not my first choice, but it works in a pinch and is handy when you need to touch up a panel after a repair.)

Cementing is a messy process, best done outside or in your garage. Because you will be working with dusty powders, you **must** work in a well-ventilated area and wear a respirator or dust mask.

Tools for Cementing
2 natural fiber nail brushes
    or 2 small scrub brushes
A mixing container
Stir stick
Wooden chopstick or dowel
    sharpened in a pencil
    sharpener
Respirator or dust mask

Formula Ingredients
4 parts whiting (chalk dust)
2 parts plaster of Paris
1-1/2 parts turpentine
1 part boiled linseed oil
1 part portland cement
Optional: Powdered lamp
    black or grout colorant (to
    color)

Other Supplies
Additional whiting
Newspapers

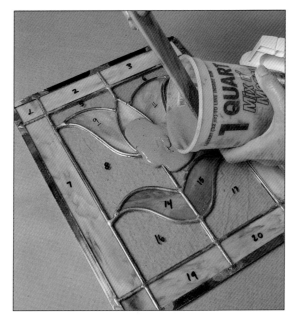

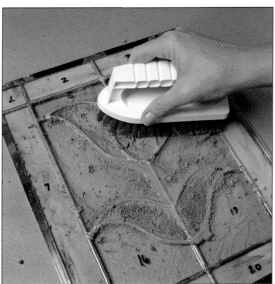

1. Cover your work table with newspapers or kraft paper. Make sure the surface is smooth and free of debris so you won't crack your glass while you work.

Mix your cement using the ingredients listed previously. Mix enough for about one pint of cement.

Place ingredients in a container. *Option:* Sprinkle lamp black or colorant over the ingredients. Using the stir stick, mix to a consistency of mayonnaise. Add whiting to thicken; add turpentine to thin. *Or* purchase pre-mixed cement.

Place your panel on the covered work table and pour the cement mixture on the panel.

2. Work the mixture around the panel, using a brush in a circular motion. Be sure to push it under the face of the came, filling in any gaps or spaces around the glass and cames. Wipe off any excess cement with the edge of your cement brush.

3. Sprinkle a light dusting of whiting over the panel.

4. Using a clean brush, repeat the same circular motion. The whiting dries up excess moisture, helps clean the glass, and creates a natural patina from the lead came to color the solder joints. The more you work, the more beautiful your project will become. Sweep off the remaining whiting. Sprinkle with a second light dusting of whiting and brush again.

5. Use a chopstick, sharpened wooden dowel, or a fid to "dress the came" by removing all excess cement from the panel. Try to create a clean edge around each piece of came.

Change the paper on your work table, turn over the panel, and repeat the entire cementing process on the other side. When you have cemented both sides, allow the panel to lay flat on a clean, dry surface for at least 24 hours. (I like to allow at least 48 hours for the cement on a large panel to set and cure.)

When the cement is dry, it's time for the final cleanup. Clean your glass with whiting and a soft cloth and/or soap and water. Go easy with the water. A coffee filter makes an excellent drying cloth—it doesn't leave lint or fuzz behind. Projects that have not been cemented can be freely washed with soap and water.

Step 7 • Adding a Patina

Depending on the color of the came you are working with, you may wish to apply patina to the solder joints or use a paint pen to color the joints so they blend better with the color of the came metal. Patinas are specially formulated colorants for lead. They can change silver solder joints to varying shades of copper or make them black as lead. Several brands of patinas are available at craft and metal stores.

My Recipe for Copper Patina

For years I have used this recipe to make a copper patina. After buffing with red jeweler's rouge, the metal will be a golden pink color.

4 oz. water

2 tablespoons copper sulfate (available at hardware stores)

1 tablespoon lemon juice (artificial works, too)

Apply the patina to solder joints using a cotton swab. Don't dip directly into your patina; that weakens its strength. Pour a small amount into the cap or a small container. Two or three coats may be necessary. Polish black patina with liquid auto wax. Buff copper with red jeweler's rouge, which is a available at lapidary and jewelers supply stores.

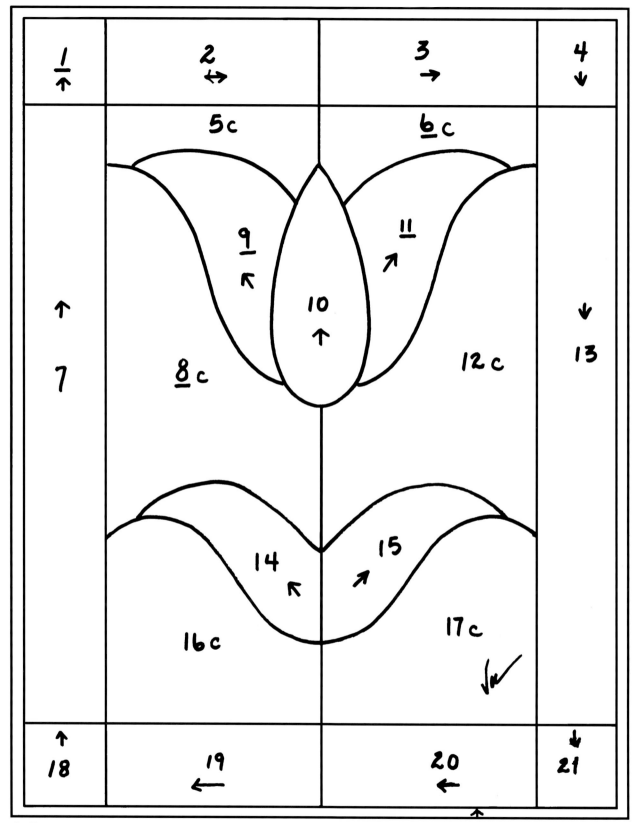

Art Nouveau Tulip Panel – Enlarge to 170% for actual size

The Projects

The projects in this section include a variety of panels, garden ornaments, boxes, tabletop accessories, and a fireplace screen.

Each project includes one or more photographs, a list of supplies you'll need, and step-by-step instructions for cutting, assembling, and finishing. The Supplies list for each project usually includes a listing for "Basic Tools"—the basic tools and supplies you will need. They are listed below.

Basic Tools & Supplies

Pattern Making Supplies:
- Pattern fixative or rubber cement
- Pencil & eraser
- Felt-tip pen or china marker
- Pattern paper
- 18" metal ruler with cork back
- Transfer paper
- Colored pencils
- Pattern shears
- Pattern paper
- Craft knife

Glass Cutting Tools:
- Glass cutter
- Cutting oil
- Carborundum stone or emery cloth
- *Optional:* Grinder
- Combination pliers
- *Optional:* Breaking pliers
- Running pliers
- Grozing pliers

Supplies for Assembling:
- Work board
- Squaring bars
- Leading knife
- Lead nippers
- Fid (lathekin)
- Lead vise
- Triangle with 45 degree and 90 degree angles
- Desk brush and dust pan
- Horseshoe nails
- Lead spacers

Soldering Tools & Supplies:
- Soldering iron with 1/4" tip
- Rheostat
- Soldering iron stand
- Tip cleaner
- Flux and flux brush
- 50/50 solder wire

Safety Gear:
- Safety glasses
- Face mask

Arts & Crafts
Lantern with Tree

This shade was made for a traditional Arts & Crafts light fixture, but almost any porch light fixture could be used to create this project. If you are working with a fixture that has removable glass panels, simply remove them. Adjust the size of the pattern to fit your fixture.

Opalescent glass works best for this project. The back (fourth) side of the lantern is made by cutting one solid piece of glass the same size as the three leaded panels. A brass plate with a center hole was soldered to the tops of the four panels.

Supplies

Glass:
1 sq. ft. green
2 sq. ft. green ripple
1/2 sq. ft. brown
2 sq. ft. honey cream

Came:
2 6-ft. strips of 3/16" U flat
3 6-ft. strips of 3/16" H round

Other Supplies:
6" x 6" brass top plate
Coffee can filled with sand *or* old books
Cementing supplies, see page 53
Optional: Patina, see page 55

Tools:
Basic Tools & Supplies as listed

Pictured on page 59

Step-by-Step

Prepare & Cut Glass:

1. Make four copies of the pattern. Number and mark the grain line on each piece. Using pattern shears, cut out the design from three copies. Trim the outer edges of the other copy of the pattern.
2. Adhere pattern pieces to the glass. Cut out each piece.
3. Use grozing pliers to remove any chips or protrusions. Smooth the edges with a grinder or carborundum stone as needed to fit the pattern.
4. Stretch the lead came.
5. For the back panel, cut a single piece of glass the finished size of the leaded panels.

Lead Up, Solder & Cement:

1. On your work board, tape or pin the remaining uncut copy of the pattern. Lay out the cut pieces of glass on the work board.
2. Lead up one tree panel, working from one corner, placing a piece of lead, a piece of glass, and so on, until all pieces are in place. Use the grinder to smooth edges of the glass and make adjustments. Each piece must fit the pattern lines.
3. Solder the joints on the top.
4. Turn project over and solder the joints on the back.
5. Repeat steps 2, 3, and 4 to complete the other two leaded panels.
6. Wrap the back panel in one piece of U-shaped came. Solder the top joint.
7. Cement all four panels. Let set and cure. Clean.

Assemble & Finish:

You are building a four-sided glass box.

1. Stand the back glass panel on its bottom edge. Support it with books or a coffee can filled with sand. Place one of the leaded panels at a right angle to the back and solder in place.
2. Add the remaining panels one at a time to assemble all four sides, forming a box. Use a framing triangle or square to make sure the box is square.
3. Solder the top edges and down the inside seams of the box.
4. Fit the brass panel on top of the four sides and solder in place. Be sure the brass plate is securely attached to the glass sides. *Option:* If you are using another type of fixture, attach the hardware at this time.
5. Clean up the panels.
6. *Option:* Apply patina. Let dry.
7. Install. ❖

Arts & Crafts Lantern with Tree – Actual size

Art Deco Lantern

Only one side of this lantern features the art deco design; the other three panels are solid pieces of cream opalescent glass. If you would like to make all four sides decorative, you will need to purchase additional materials.

The lantern can be made with or without its decorative roof. You can use almost any hanging fixture top to complete the lantern.

Supplies

Glass:
Cream opalescent, 13" x 18"
Green opalescent, 6" x 6"
Pink opalescent, 4" x 4"
Small piece of gold opalescent

Came:
2 6-ft. strips of 1/8" U zinc
1 6-ft. strip of 1/8" H lead

Other Supplies:
6" x 6" brass top plate
Coffee can filled with sand *or* old books
Cementing supplies, see page 53
Optional: Lantern top

Tools:
Basic Tools & Supplies as listed
Came notcher *or* wire cutters

Step-by-Step

Prepare & Cut Glass:
1. Make two copies of the pattern. Number and mark the grain line on each piece. Using pattern shears, cut out design from one copy. Trim the outer edges of the other copy of the pattern.
2. Adhere pattern pieces to the glass. Cut out each piece.
3. Use grozing pliers to remove any chips or protrusions. Smooth the edges with a grinder or carborundum stone as needed to fit the pattern.
4. Stretch the lead came.

Lead Up, Solder & Cement:
1. On your work board, tape or pin the second copy of the pattern. Lay out the cut pieces of glass on the work board.
2. Cut the 1/8" U-shaped zinc came to frame each glass panel (both plain and leaded), using a came notcher or wire cutters. *If you are using a notcher,* measure the length of each side of the panel, mark the measurements along the top edge of a piece of zinc came, and notch all four corners of the came. *If you are using wire cutters,* cut four strips of zinc came to fit each of the four sides.
3. To assemble the leaded panel, place the notched or cut zinc came in the corner of your work board. Insert the first corner piece of glass.
4. Lead up the panel, using 1/8" H-shaped lead came.
5. When the glass pieces are in place, wrap the rest of the U-shaped zinc came around the top and other side of the panel. Hold in place with pushpins. Make sure the panel is square and on pattern.
6. Solder all the leaded joints. Turn the panel over and solder the joints on the back.
7. Wrap the three unleaded panels in zinc came. Solder the ends of the zinc came together. *Option:* If you are making four leaded panels, build the other three sides the same way.
8. Cement the panels. Let set and cure. Clean.

Assemble:
1. Use an empty coffee can filled with sand or books to hold the panels in place or get a friend to help. Place the panels together at right angles. Make sure they are square, then solder the top edges together.
2. Gently turn the project over. Solder the bottom edges together at the corners.

continued on page 64

continued from page 62

3. Place the shade on its side, supporting it with books. Run a smooth solder seam along each inside corner. (This gives your shade lots of strength and support.)

4. *If you are using a brass top plate,* position it on top of the four-sided shade and solder it in place. *If you are using another type of hanging fixture,* attach its hardware to the shade.

5. Clean up the panels.

6. *Optional:* Apply patina. (I used black patina to match the top of the fixture.) Let dry. ❖

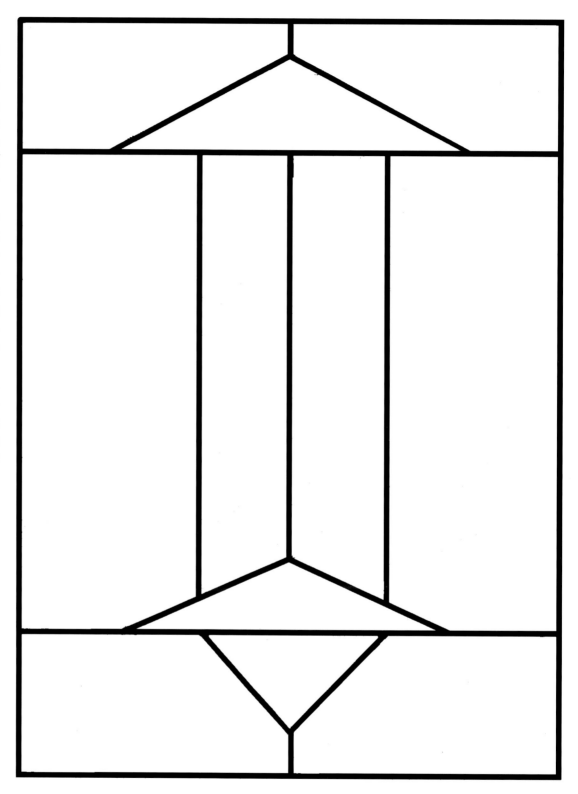

Art Deco Lantern pattern, shown actual size

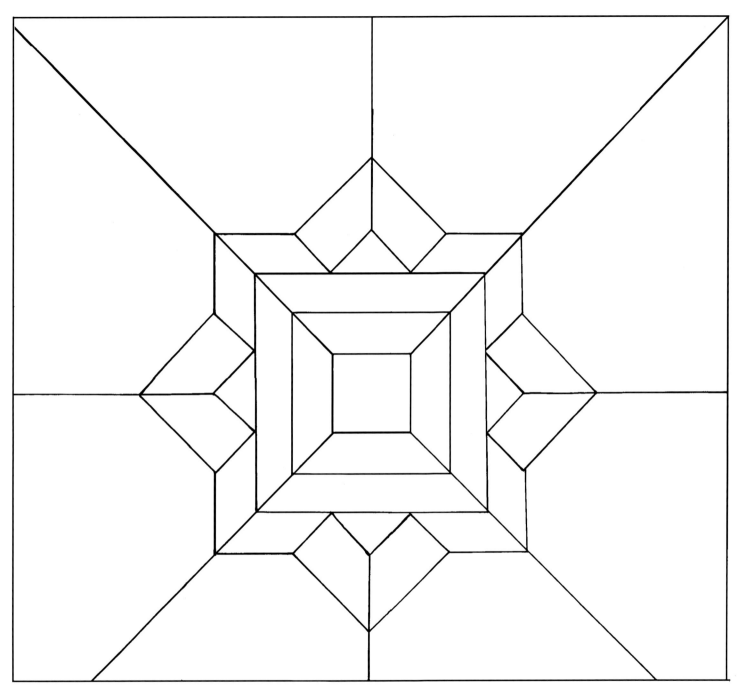

*Bevel Cluster Cabinet Door pattern – Enlarge to 243% for actual size.
Instructions on page 66*

*NOTE: The center bevel cluster is available already put together. If you
cannot find one exactly like it, feel free to choose a bevel medallion
cluster that would fit your project.*

Bevel Cluster
Cabinet Door

I used a bevel cluster to make a panel for this cabinet door. You will find wonderful bevel cluster designs at your local stained glass shop or on the Internet. You can also make the panel using any type or color of art glass instead of beveled ones.

Pattern on page 65

Size: 15" x 19"

Supplies

Glass:
2 sq. ft. clear textured
1 bevel cluster *or* 2 sq. ft. art glass

Came:
3 6-ft. strips of 3/16" H brass
1 6-ft. strip of 1/8" U brass

Other Supplies:
Gold paint pen

Tools:
Basic Tools & Supplies as listed
Hacksaw *or* power came saw

Step-by-Step

Prepare & Cut Glass:
1. Make two copies of the pattern. Number and mark the grain line on each piece. Using pattern shears, cut out design from one copy. Trim the outer edges of the other copy of the pattern.
2. Adhere pattern pieces to the glass. Cut out each piece.
3. Use grozing pliers to remove any chips or protrusions from the pieces you cut. Smooth the edges with a grinder or carborundum stone as needed to fit the pattern.

Lead Up & Solder:
Brass came panels are built just like leaded ones. Use a hacksaw or power came saw to cut the brass came to size.
1. On your work board, tape or pin the second copy of the pattern. Lay out the cut pieces of glass on the work board.
2. Lead up the panel, working from one corner, placing a piece of came, a piece of glass, and so on, until all pieces are in place. Use the grinder to smooth edges of the glass and make adjustments. Each piece must fit the pattern lines.
3. Solder the joints on the top.
4. Turn project over and solder the joints on the back.

Finish:
1. Cement and clean the panel.
2. Use a gold paint pen to color the solder joints to match the brass came.
3. Install the panel in the cabinet door. ❖

Candle Cubes

Make one or a dozen of these stackable candle cubes. They make great gifts or party centerpieces. I used peach colored mirror in the bottom of the cube. It is available at stained glass stores. If you are using silver mirror you will may want to use zinc or brass came instead of copper.

Supplies

For each cube

Glass:
4 clear bevels, 3" x 3"
1 piece peach-colored mirror, 3" x 3"

Came:
1 6-ft. strip 1/8" U copper

Other Supplies:
Copper patina, see page 55

Tools:
Basic Tools & Supplies
Came notcher

Step-by-Step

1. Use a notcher to miter the corners of the came or cut with nippers.
2. Wrap the mirror piece in came. Solder the corner joint.
3. Wrap the four bevels in came. Solder the corner joints.
4. Form a square with the four wrapped bevels. Tack solder the upper and lower corner edges.
5. Set this assembly on top of the wrapped mirror square. Solder the corners.
6. *Option:* If you want to stack your candle cubes, arrange them and tack solder any spots where the cames touch.
7. Clean up with soap and water.
8. Apply copper patina to the soldered joints. ❖

Candle Cube Tips

- Use glass votive cups to hold the candles rather than putting candles in the candle cubes.

- If you stack the cubes, don't burn a candle under any cube. The heat will crack the glass.

Cigar Sign

Size: 5-1/2" x 18-1/2"

Supplies

Glass:
1 sq. ft. red
1 sq. ft. green
1 sq. ft. yellow
4 blue jewels

Came:
3 6-ft. strips of 1/8" H lead
1 6-ft. strip of U zinc

Other Supplies:
Cementing supplies, see page 53

Tools:
Basic Tools & Supplies as listed
Came notcher

Step-by-Step

Prepare & Cut Glass:

1. Make two copies of the pattern. Number and mark the grain line on each piece. Using pattern shears, cut out design from one copy. Trim the outer edges of the other copy of the pattern.
2. Adhere pattern pieces to the glass. Cut out each piece.
3. Use grozing pliers to remove any chips or protrusions on the glass pieces. Smooth the edges with a grinder or carborundum stone as needed to fit the pattern.
4. Stretch the lead came.

Lead Up & Solder:

1. On your work board, tape or pin the second copy of the pattern. Lay out the cut pieces of glass on the work board.
2. Lead up the panel, working from one corner, placing a piece of lead, a piece of glass, and so on, until all pieces are in place. Use the grinder to smooth edges of the glass and make adjustments. Each piece must fit the pattern lines.
3. Solder the joints on the top.
4. Turn project over and solder the joints on the back.

Finish:

1. Cement and clean the panel.
2. Use a notcher to miter the corners of the zinc came or cut with nippers.
3. Wrap the panel with zinc came. Solder the joint. ❖

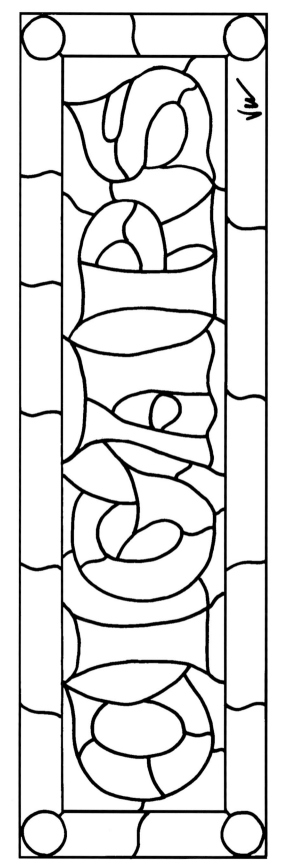

*Cigar Sign pattern
Enlarge to 210%
for actual size*

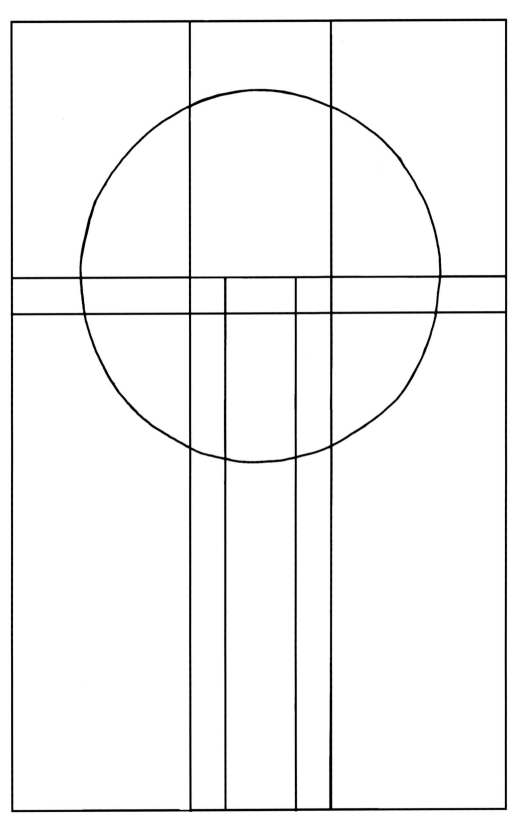

Contemporary Brass Panel Enlarge to 262% for actual size

Instructions on page 74.

Contemporary Brass Panel

Clear textured panels are a good choice for decorating a contemporary setting. In this panel that's easy enough for a beginner, I used three different clear textured glasses and small bevels.

Building a panel with brass came is the same as building a panel with lead came, except you will need to cut the came with a hacksaw or power came saw. Using a came bender makes it easier to shape the came to fit the circle in the center of the panel.

Pattern on page 73

Size 14" x 21-1/2"

Supplies

Glass:
2 bevels, 1" x 1"
3 sq. ft. clear granite back
1 sq. ft. clear iridized waterglass
1 sq. ft. clear textured

Came:
3 6-ft. strips of 3/16" H brass
2 6-ft. strips of 3/8" U brass

Other Supplies:
2 eye hooks
Gold paint pen
Cementing supplies , see page 53

Tools:
Basic Tools & Supplies as listed
Came bender
Hacksaw *or* power came saw

Step-by-Step

Prepare & Cut Glass:
1. Make two copies of the pattern. Number and mark the grain line on each piece. Using pattern shears, cut out design from one copy. Trim the outer edges of the other copy of the pattern.
2. Adhere pattern pieces to the glass. Cut out each piece.
3. Use grozing pliers to remove any chips or protrusions on the glass pieces. Smooth the edges with a grinder or carborundum stone as needed to fit the pattern.
4. Cut the U-shaped brass came. Miter the bottom corners but cut the top intersections straight so they can accept the eye hooks.

Lead Up & Solder:
1. On your work board, tape or pin the second copy of the pattern. Lay out the cut pieces of glass on the work board.
2. Lead up the panel, working from one corner, placing a piece of came, a piece of glass, and so on, until all pieces are in place. Use the grinder to smooth edges of the glass and make adjustments. Each piece must fit the pattern lines.
3. Solder the joints on the top side of the panel.
4. Turn project over and solder the joints on the back.

Finish:
1. Insert eyehooks in the open ends of the perimeter came. Solder in place.
2. Cement and clean the panel.
3. Paint the solder joints with a gold paint pen. ❖

Contemporary Dichroic Panel

This decorative panel is made using several different dichroic glasses. Dichroic glass has had a special coating applied to it at the factory. The coating is permanent and makes the glass change colors as the light hits it. It's expensive, but if you like the effect it's worth the investment. (Of course, you could use this design with colored glass instead.)

Pattern on page 78

Size: 9" x 20"

Supplies

Glass:
2 sq. ft. assorted dichroic glasses
2 sq. ft. clear waterglass
10 clear bevels, 1" x 1"

Came:
3 6-ft. strips of 1/8" H lead
1 6-ft. strip of 3/8" H lead (for the perimeter)

Other Supplies:
Optional: Black metal frame

Tools:
Basic Tools & Supplies as listed

Step-by-Step

Prepare & Cut Glass:
1. Make two copies of the pattern. Number and mark the grain line on each piece. Using pattern shears, cut out design from one copy. Trim the outer edges of the other copy of the pattern.
2. Adhere pattern pieces to the glass. Cut out each piece.
3. Use grozing pliers to remove any chips or protrusions on the glass pieces. Smooth the edges with a grinder or carborundum stone as needed to fit the pattern.
4. Stretch the lead came.

Lead Up & Solder:
1. On your work board, tape or pin the second copy of the pattern. Lay out the cut pieces of glass on the work board.
2. Lead up the panel, working from one corner, placing a piece of lead, a piece of glass, and so on, until all pieces are in place. Use the grinder to smooth edges of the glass and make adjustments. Each piece must fit the pattern lines.
3. Solder the joints on the top.
4. Turn project over and solder the joints on the back.

Finish:
1. Cement and clean the panel.
2. *Option:* Place panel in a black frame. ❖

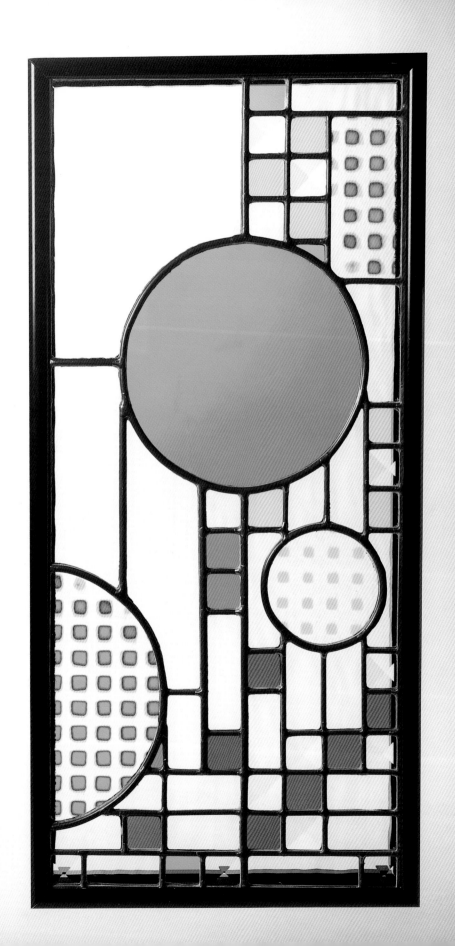

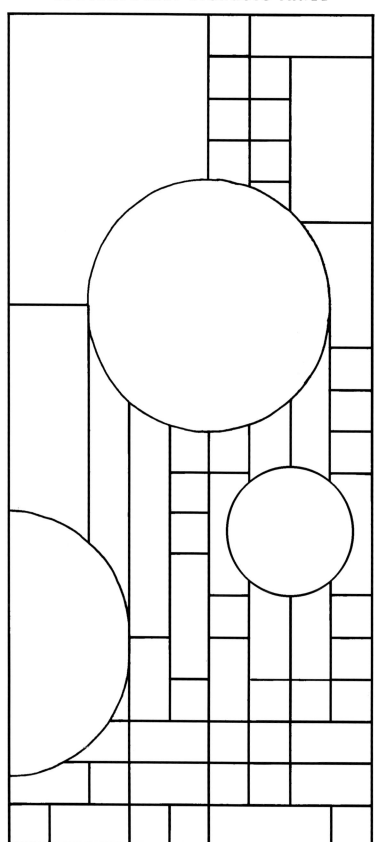

*Contemporary Dichroic Panel
Enlarge to 236% for actual size*

Instructions on page 76

Jumping Bass pattern
Enlarge to 171% for actual size

Instructions on page 80

Jumping Bass Panel

A perfect gift for fishers!

Pattern on page 79

Size: 11" x 14"

Supplies

Glass:
1-1/2 sq. ft. blue waterglass
1 sq. ft. streaky blue
1/2 sq. ft. lighter blue
1/2 sq. ft. white iridized
1/2 sq. ft. white
1 sq. ft. mossy green
1 sq. ft. lighter green

Came:
3 6-ft. strips of 1/8" H lead
1 6-ft. strip 3/8" H lead

Other supplies:
Cementing supplies, see page 53
Frame

Tools:
Basic tools and supplies as listed

Step-by-Step

Prepare & Cut Glass:
1. Make two copies of the pattern. Number and mark the grain line on each piece. Using pattern shears, cut out design from one copy. Trim the outer edges of the other copy of the pattern.
2. Adhere pattern pieces to the glass. Cut out each piece.
3. Use grozing pliers to remove any chips or protrusions on the glass pieces. Smooth the edges with a grinder or carborundum stone as needed to fit the pattern.
4. Stretch the lead came.

Lead Up & Solder:
1. On your work board, tape or pin the second copy of the pattern. Lay out the cut pieces of glass on the work board.
2. Lead up the panel, working from one corner, placing a piece of lead, a piece of glass, and so on, until all pieces are in place. Use the grinder to smooth edges of the glass and make adjustments. Each piece must fit the pattern lines.
3. Solder the joints on the top.
4. Turn project over and solder the joints on the back.

Finish:
Cement and clean the panel. ❖

Garden Buddies

Use these colorful, whimsical glass ornaments to brighten your garden or indoor plants—use them in containers or right out in your flower garden. They also could be used as sun catchers by eliminating the brass rod stake and attaching wire loops. You could then hang them from hooks or monofilament line.

These projects are put together like copper foil projects, where each piece of glass is wrapped with metal, but U-shaped lead came (instead of foil) is used to wrap the glass.

Ladybug

See pattern on page 87
Size: 7" x 5"

Supplies

Glass:
Red, 8" x 8"
1 large black glass nugget

Came:
1 6-ft. strip of 1/8" U lead

Other Supplies:
Brass rod, 1/4" diameter, 36" long (for stand)
14 gauge copper wire
Black glass paint
Small artist's paint brush (you'll use the handle end)

Tools:
Basic Tools & Supplies as listed
Needlenose pliers

Step-by-Step

Prepare & Cut Glass:

1. Make two copies of the pattern. Number and mark the grain line on each piece. Using pattern shears, cut out design from one copy. Trim the outer edges of the other copy of the pattern.
2. Adhere pattern pieces to the glass. Cut out each piece.
3. Use grozing pliers to remove any chips or protrusions on the glass pieces. Smooth the edges with a grinder or carborundum stone as needed to fit the pattern.
4. Stretch the lead came.

Assemble:

1. Place the second copy of the pattern on a Homasote work board.
2. Wrap each piece of glass and the nugget in U-shaped came.
3. Place each wrapped piece on top of the pattern. Secure with pushpins.
4. Solder together each lead joint. It may be necessary to add additional solder along some seams to provide additional support; then sol-der the joints and places where the came intersects.

Finish:

1. Cut six 2" pieces of wire for the legs. Solder to the sides of the ladybug as shown on the pattern to form legs. Bend to shape.
2. Cut a 4" piece of wire. Make the antennae by forming small loops at the two ends of the wire. Fill the loops with solder. Bend the wire in half and solder to the top of the black nugget.
3. Dip the handle end of a small paint brush in black glass paint and touch to the glass surface. (The handle will make perfectly round black dots.) Let dry.
4. Bend the end of the brass rod over about 1" to form a right angle. Attach this end to the back of the ladybug by soldering it firmly to the lead came. *Tip:* Don't be shy with the solder. You want this connection to be really strong.
5. Clean with soap and water. ❖

Pond Frog

Size: 9" x 6"

Supplies

Glass:
Green, 8" x 8"
Yellow, 8"x 8"

Came:
2 6-ft. strips of 1/8" U lead

Other Supplies:
Brass rod, 1/4" diameter, 36" long (for stand)

Tools:
Basic Tools & Supplies as listed
Needlenose pliers

Step-by-Step

Prepare & Cut Glass:

1. Make two copies of the pattern. Number and mark the grain line on each piece. Using pattern shears, cut out design from one copy. Trim the outer edges of the other copy of the pattern.
2. Adhere pattern pieces to the glass. Cut out each piece.
3. Use grozing pliers to remove any chips or protrusions on the glass pieces. Smooth the edges with a grinder or carborundum stone as needed to fit the pattern.
4. Stretch the lead came.

Assemble:

1. Place the second copy of the pattern on a Homasote work board.
2. Wrap each piece of glass in U-shaped came.
3. Place each wrapped piece on top of your pattern and secure with pushpins. Solder together each lead joint and at outside intersections.

Finish:

1. Bend the end of the brass rod over about 1" to form a right angle. Attach this end to the back of the frog by soldering it firmly to the lead came face. *Tip:* Don't be shy with the solder, but make your solder connection nice and smooth. You want this connection to be really strong.
2. Clean with soap and water. ❖

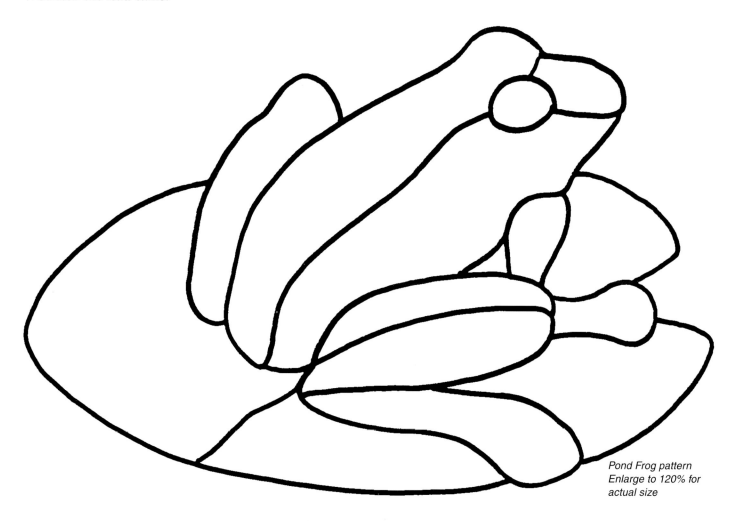

Pond Frog pattern
Enlarge to 120% for
actual size

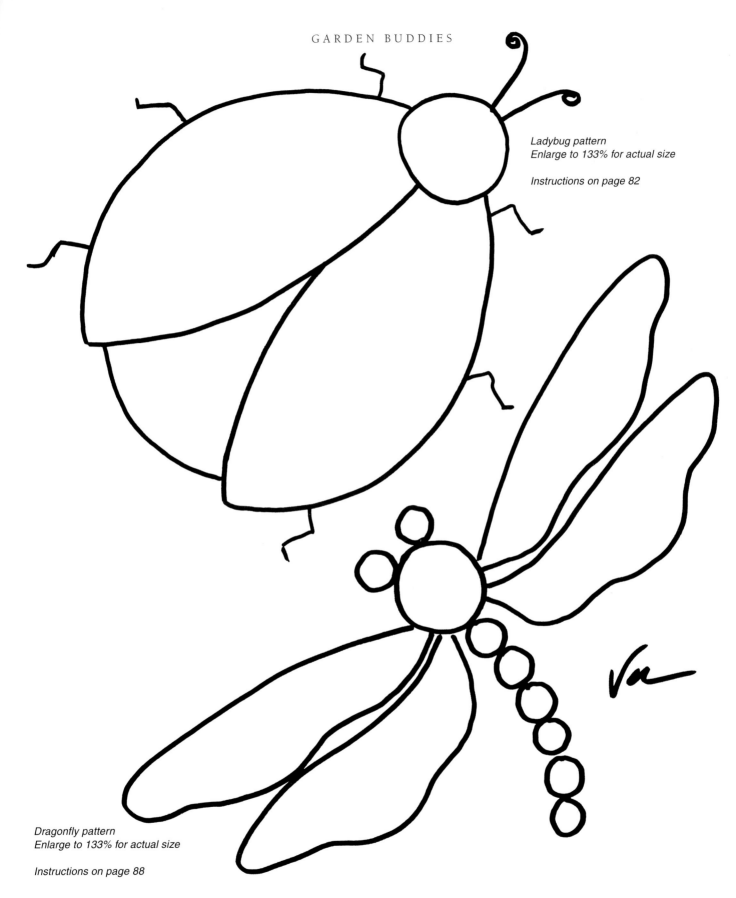

*Ladybug pattern
Enlarge to 133% for actual size*

Instructions on page 82

*Dragonfly pattern
Enlarge to 133% for actual size*

Instructions on page 88

Dragonfly

Pattern on page 87

Size: 11" x 6"

Supplies

Glass:
White iridescent, 8" x 8"
7 small iridescent blue nuggets (about 1/2" diameter)
1 large dark blue nugget (about 1-1/4" diameter)

Came:
2 6-ft. strips of 1/8" U lead

Other Supplies:
Brass rod, 1/4" diameter, 36" long (for stand)

Tools:
Basic Tools & Supplies as listed
Needlenose pliers

Step-by-Step

Prepare & Cut Glass:

1. Make two copies of the pattern. Number and mark the grain line on each piece. Using pattern shears, cut out design from one copy. Trim the outer edges of the other copy of the pattern.
2. Adhere pattern pieces to the glass. Cut out each piece.
3. Use grozing pliers to remove any chips or protrusions on the glass pieces. Smooth the edges with a grinder or carborundum stone as needed to fit the pattern.
4. Stretch the lead came.

Assemble:

1. Place the second copy of the pattern on a Homasote work board.
2. Wrap each piece of glass in U-shaped came.
3. Place each wrapped piece on top of the pattern and secure with pushpins. Make sure the came intersections on each nugget are placed against the next nugget. (This will give you smooth outside edges.) Solder together each lead joint and at the intersections.

Finish:

1. Bend the end of the brass rod over about 1" to form a right angle. Attach this end to the back of the frog by soldering it firmly to the lead came face. *Tip: Don't be shy with the solder, but make your solder connection nice and smooth. You want this connection to be really strong.*
2. Clean with soap and water. ❖

Berry & Vine Lantern

This woodsy lighting fixture was inspired by the Arts & Crafts movement of the early 20th century. The leaded glass vine simply wraps around the outside of the lantern-style lighting fixture.

You can adapt this technique to just about any lighting fixture whether it has a wood or metal frame. If your fixture has glass panels you like, you can keep them and skip cutting and installing new glass.

Panel size: 7-3/8" x 6-7/8"

Supplies

Glass:
Leaf green opalescent, 6" x 6"
5 small assorted amber nuggets
Optional: Cream opalescent, 22" x 8"
  (to cut new panels for fixture)

Came:
1 6-ft. strip of 1/8" U shaped lead

Other Supplies:
Copper patina, se page 55
Silicone adhesive

Tools:
Basic Tools & Supplies as listed

Step-by-Step

Prepare & Cut Glass:
1. Coat lead came with copper patina. Let dry.
2. Make two copies of the pattern. Number and mark the grain line on each piece. Cut out design from one copy.
3. Adhere pattern pieces to the glass. Cut out the leaves.
4. Use grozing pliers to remove any chips or protrusions on the glass pieces. Smooth the edges with a grinder or carborundum stone as needed to fit the pattern.
5. *Option:* Cut new glass panels to fit your lighting fixture. Install them in the fixture.
6. Stretch the lead came.

Assemble:
1. Wrap leaves in patinaed came, leaving one side 2-3" long.
2. Wrap nuggets in patinaed came. Solder intersections.
3. Clean up nuggets with glass cleaner.

4. Starting at the back corner edge of the side glass panel, apply a dab of clear silicone to the glass and fixture frame. Place the end of the remaining patinaed came (it will be the vine) over the silicone and tape in place. Using the photo as a guide, gently mold and wrap the strip of came around the fixture. Use tape to hold the "vine" in place while you work.
5. When you are happy with the placement of the vine, add the wrapped leaves and nuggets. Trim the excess lead as necessary.
6. Solder the leaves and nuggets to the came vine.
7. Gently lift the edges of the leaves and apply more silicone to secure the vine to the background glass.

Finish:
1. Touch up any visible solder joints with copper patina.
2. Let dry 24 hours. Remove any excess silicone with a craft knife.
3. Clean glass with glass cleaner and soft rag. ❖

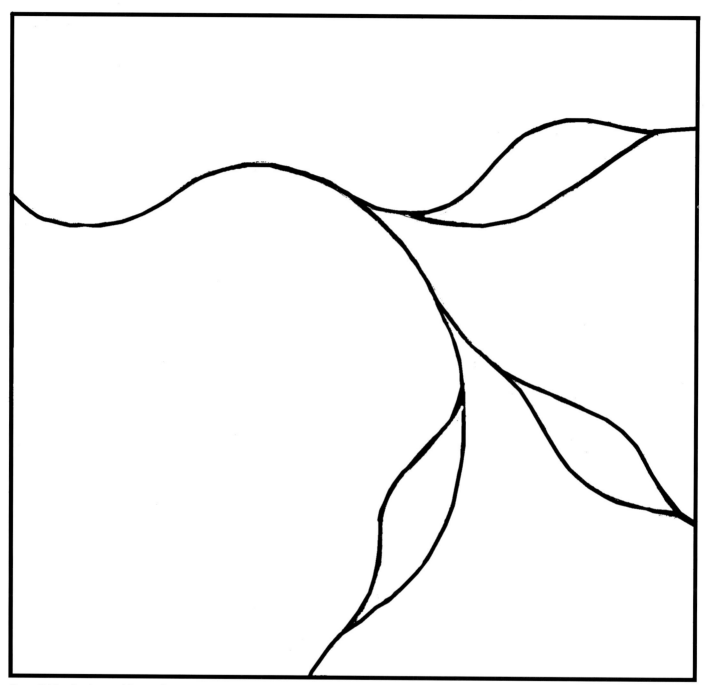

Berry & Vine Lantern - side panel
Actual size

Berry & Vine Lantern - front panel
Actual size

Garden Birdhouse

This birdhouse can be used inside or outside. Because it is built with brass came and lead free solder, it is bird friendly.

Size: 8" x 4" x 7"

Supplies

Glass:
Bluish purple streaky, 14" x 18"

Came:
2 6-ft. strips of 1/8" U brass

Other Supplies:
5" x 13" sheet of brass for roof, 1/16" thick (available at hardware or hobby stores—if you can't find brass sheet that is 13" long, you can piece the roof from four 4" panels of brass)
10" copper foil, 3/16" wide
12 gauge copper wire
Copper/green patina
Gold paint pen

Tools:
Basic Tools & Supplies as listed
Came notcher

Step-by-Step

Prepare & Cut:

1. Make two copies of the pattern. Number and mark the grain line on each piece. Using pattern shears, cut out design from one copy. Trim the outer edges of the other copy of the pattern.
2. Adhere pattern pieces to the glass. Cut out each piece.
3. Use grozing pliers to remove any chips or protrusions on the glass pieces. Smooth the edges with a grinder or carborundum stone as needed to fit the pattern.

Assemble:

1. Wrap each piece of glass in 1/8" U-shaped brass came, using a notcher to cut corner angles or cut with wire nippers. Solder joints where came meets.
2. Wrap the hole on the front of the birdhouse with copper foil. Brush with flux and tin (coat) with solder.
3. Assemble sides and floor of birdhouse as shown in Fig. 1. Solder together all corners and run a solder bead along all sides of the floor panel to make it waterproof and strong.
4. Bend brass sheet in half and position on roof. (You should have 1/2" overhang on the front and back and 1-1/2" on sides.)
5. Drill two holes in the center of the roof for the wire hanger. Slip the wire through and twist or curly securely.
6. Cut two 1-3/4" long pieces of U-shaped brass came. Slip them together to form a square. Solder on front of birdhouse for a perch.

Finish:

1. Paint the foil around the birdhouse hole and all solder joints with the gold paint pen.
2. Use a paintbrush to apply several coats of copper/green patina to the roof and to lead. Follow the manufacturer's instructions for best results. Let dry completely.
3. Clean birdhouse with soap and water. ❖

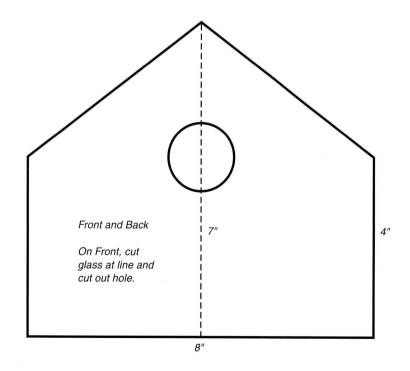

Front and Back

7"

4"

On Front, cut glass at line and cut out hole.

8"

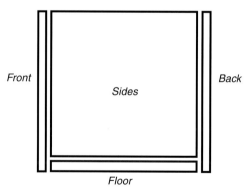

Front

Sides

Back

Floor

Fig. 1 - Sectional View

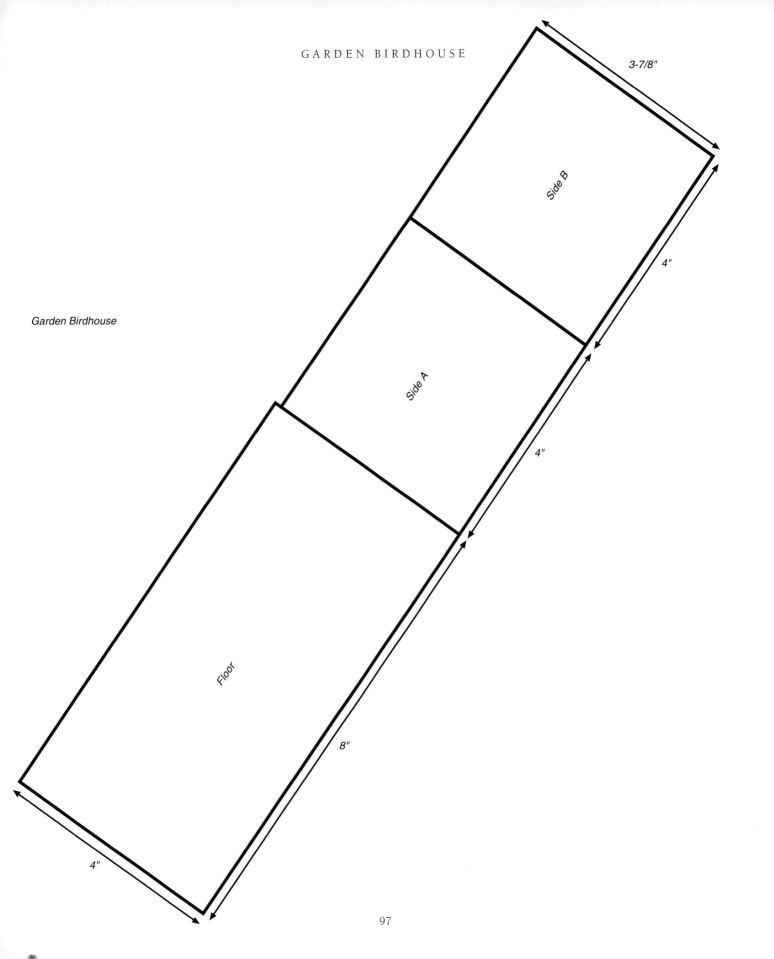

Garden Birdhouse

3-7/8"

Side B

4"

Side A

4"

Floor

8"

4"

Cape Lookout Lighthouse Panel

This panel would be wonderful for a beach house or any place you wish to evoke the sea and the surf. To save time, the window muntins on the lighthouse are created by an overlay of copper foil sheet.

Size: 8" x 23"

Supplies

Glass:
2 sq. ft. black
1 sq. ft. white
White wispy, 6" x 6"
Blue waterglass, 24" x 18"
Green, 8" x 8"
Brown, 6" x 6"
1 small black nugget

Came:
3 6-ft. strips of 1/8" H lead
1 6-ft. strip of 1/4" U zinc
Optional: 4" of 3/8" H lead

Other Supplies:
2 eye hooks
6" x 6" piece of copper foil sheet
Cement, see page 53
Patina, see page 55

Tools:
Basic Tools & Supplies as listed

Step-by-Step

Prepare & Cut Glass:
1. Make two copies of the pattern. Number and mark the grain line on each piece. Using pattern shears, cut out design from one copy. Trim the outer edges of the other copy of the pattern.
2. Adhere pattern pieces to the glass. Cut out each piece.
3. Use grozing pliers to remove any chips or protrusions on the glass pieces. Smooth the edges with a grinder or carborundum stone as needed to fit the pattern.
4. Stretch the lead came.

Make the Overlays:
1. Cover the fronts of the two large window pieces with copper foil sheeting. Burnish it tightly to the glass. Fold the edges around to the back and trim excess.
2. Transfer the design from the pattern to the surface of the foil using carbon paper or just the pressure from your pencil.
3. Cut out the design, using a sharp craft knife. Take care not to cut through any of the intersections. You want to end up with filigree

that is connected at every point. (They will look like lace or a spider web. When you are leading up your window treat these two pieces the same as any other piece.)

Lead Up & Solder:
1. On your work board, tape or pin the second copy of the pattern. Lay out the cut pieces of glass on the work board.
2. Use a hacksaw or came saw to cut the zinc came for the perimeter. **Do not** miter the corners; instead, make butt joints or flat joints. Let the side strips of zinc came extend the entire height of the panel so the ends of the zinc channel will be open and accessible for eye hooks.
3. Lead up the panel, working from one corner, placing a piece of lead, a piece of glass, and so on, until all pieces are in place. Use the grinder to smooth edges of the glass and make adjustments. Each piece must fit the pattern lines.
4. Solder the joints on the top.
5. Flux the filigree and coat with solder. You will want to build up the solder so it looks like came. When you are finished, it will look like

continued on page 100

continued from page 98

you cut and leaded 32 individual pieces instead of just two.

6. Turn project over and solder the joints on the back.

7. To make windows on the lighthouse tower, cut the face off of the scraps of 3/8" H lead. Trim to size and solder in place.

Finish:

1. Slip two eye hooks in the top open channel of the zinc perimeter came and solder in place.

2. Cement and clean the panel.

3. Apply patina. Let dry. ❖

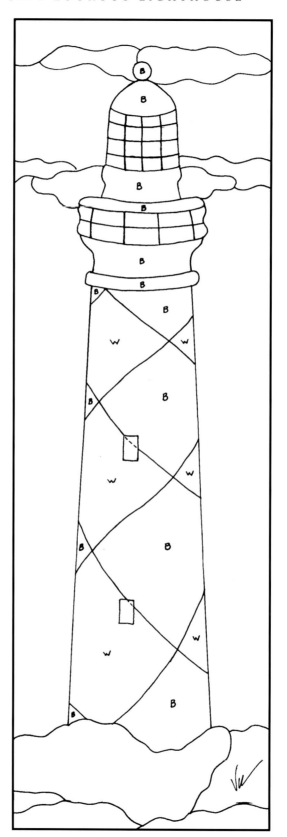

Cape Lookout Lighthouse
Enlarge to 267% for actual size

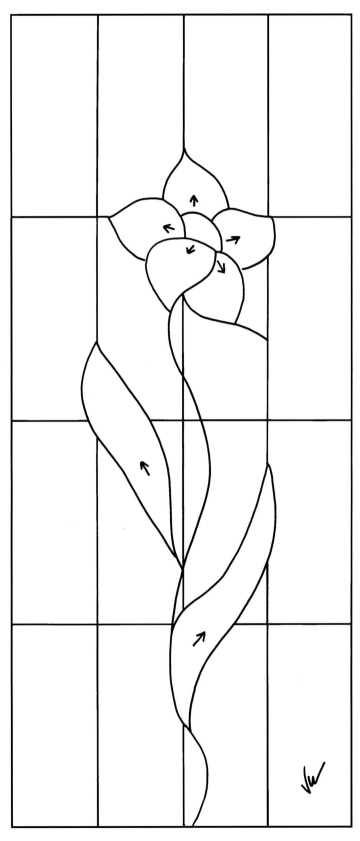

Purple Tulip Panel
Enlarge to 333%

Instructions on page 102

Purple Tulip Panel

This full-blown tulip would make a colorful accent or cabinet door.
The flower's curvy stem is formed by lead came.

Pattern on page 101

Size 12" x 28"

Supplies

Glass:
3 sq. ft. of yellow wispy
1 sq. ft. of purple
1 sq. ft. of green

Came:
4 6-ft. strips of 3/16" H lead
2 6-ft. strips of 1/8" U zinc

Tools & Supplies:
Cementing supplies, see page 53
Basic Tools & Supplies as listed

Step-by-Step

Prepare & Cut Glass:
1. Make two copies of the pattern. Number and mark the grain line on each piece. Using pattern shears, cut out design from one copy. Trim the outer edges of the other copy of the pattern.
2. Adhere pattern pieces to the glass. Cut out each piece.
3. Use grozing pliers to remove any chips or protrusions on the glass pieces. Smooth the edges with a grinder or carborundum stone as needed to fit the pattern.
4. Stretch the lead came.

Lead Up & Solder:
1. On your work board, tape or pin the second copy of the pattern. Lay out the cut pieces of glass on the work board.
2. Lead up the panel, working from one corner, placing a piece of lead, a piece of glass, and so on, until all pieces are in place. Use the grinder to smooth edges of the glass and make adjustments. Each piece must fit the pattern lines.
3. Solder the joints on the top.
4. Turn project over and solder the joints on the back.

Finish:
Cement and clean the panel. ❖

Man in the Moon Box

Supplies

Glass:
Black opalescent, 10" x 16"
Yellow opalescent, 6" x 6"
White iridized, 6" x 8"

Came:
1 6-ft. strip of 1/8" H lead
2 6-ft. strips of 1/8" H lead

Other Supplies:
4 brass box feet
2 brass box hinges
000 steel wool

Tools:
Basic Tools & Supplies as listed
Needlenose pliers

Step-by-Step

Prepare & Cut Glass:

1. Make two copies of the pattern. Number and mark the grain line on each piece. Using pattern shears, cut out design for the top from one copy. Trim the outer edges of the other copy of the pattern for the top.
2. Adhere pattern pieces to the glass. Cut out each piece.
3. For the sides, cut two strips of black glass, each 7-3/16" x 1-1/2", and two strips, each 4-3/4" x 1-1/2". For the bottom, cut one piece, 7-3/16" x 5-1/4".
4. Use grozing pliers to remove any chips or protrusions on the glass pieces. Smooth the edges with a grinder or carborundum stone as needed to fit the pattern.
5. Stretch the lead came.

Lead Up, Solder & Wrap:

1. On your work board, tape or pin the second copy of the pattern for the top. Lay out the cut pieces of glass on the work board.
2. Lead up the panel, working from one corner, placing a piece of lead, a piece of glass, and so on, until all pieces are in place. Use 1/8" H-shaped came for the inside and 1/8" U-shaped came for the perimeter. Use the grinder to smooth edges of the glass and make adjustments. Each piece must fit the pattern lines.
3. Solder the joints on the top.
4. Turn project over and solder the joints on the back.
5. Wrap each of the side and bottom pieces in 1/8" U-shaped came. Solder the corners.

Assemble:

Boxes are easy to assemble, but you must build them square so the top and bottom will fit the sides.

1. Use your work board with the right angle to assemble the box as shown in Fig. 1. Solder the corners.
2. Position the top panel on the box and hold in place with two large rubber bands.
3. Stand the box on its front side. Position the hinges on the top corner edges of the back of the box. Tape in place, leaving one edge exposed for soldering. Use a small paint brush to apply just a dot of flux to the edge of the hinge. Take care not to get flux in the working part of the hinge—this will keep solder from flowing into the hinge and ruining it. Working with the smallest corner of your soldering iron tip and a small amount of solder, attach the hinge to the box.
4. Remove the tape and solder the other end of the hinge to the box.
5. To attach the feet, turn the box bottom up. Position the brass feet on the corners of the box on top of the came. Hold in place with masking tape. Tack-solder them in place. Remove tape and add more solder or smooth out the seam, if needed.

Finish:

1. Rub lead and joints with steel wool to smooth out joints and make lead gleam.
2. Clean up box with soap and water. ❖

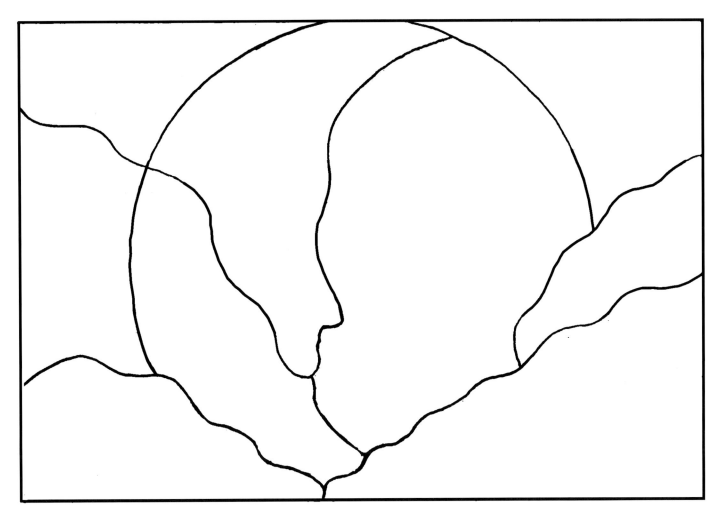

Man in the Moon Box - top
Actual size

Fig. 1 - Assembly Diagram

Nugget Buddies

Children love stained glass, and this is a great project for you to make for a child or have your children help you make. Let them wrap the nuggets and you do the soldering. No glass cutting or patterns are required.

These buddies stand up, but if you like, you could solder small wire hooks to the back and use them as sun catchers in your children's windows.

Supplies

Glass:
For the frog - 2 small and 1 large green nuggets
For the bird - 1 large and 1 small red nuggets
For the caterpillar - 11 small and 1 large nuggets

Came:
1/8" U lead

Tools:
Lead nippers
Needlenose pliers
Soldering iron
50/50 solder wire

Safety Tips for Working with Children

Always take care when working with glass and lead, especially if you are working with children.
- Be sure children are **always** supervised.
- Instruct them to **not** put lead or their fingers (after they've touched the lead) in their mouths or eyes.
- Have everyone wash his or her hands with soap and warm water after each glass project.

Step by Step

Assemble:
For the Caterpillar:
1. Lay out the 11 small nuggets to form the shape of the caterpillar.
2. Wrap each nugget in 1/8" U-shaped lead came. Place the wrapped nuggets back in their designed shape.
3. Solder at each point where the lead touches another piece of lead.
4. To make the antennae, cut a 3" piece of wire. Form a loop at each end. Fill the loop with solder. Let cool and bend in half. Solder to head.
5. To make the stand, wrap the large nugget in lead and solder the joint.
6. Lay the wrapped large nugget on your work board. Position the caterpillar on top and solder the lead intersections securely.

For the Frog:
1. Lay out nuggets to form the shape of the frog.
2. Wrap each nugget in 1/8" U-shaped lead. Place the wrapped nuggets back in their designed shape.
3. Solder at each point where the lead touches another piece of lead.
4. To make the frog's legs, cut one 6" strip of lead. Solder the center of it to the bottom of the frog's belly. Let cool.
5. Shape the lead to form the legs. Make any necessary adjustments so the frog will stand up.

For the Bird:
1. Lay out nuggets to form the shape of the bird.
2. Wrap each nugget in 1/8" U-shaped lead. Place the wrapped nuggets back in their designed shape.
3. Solder at each point where the lead touches another piece of lead.
4. To finish the bird, cut small lead strips to form the beak, tail feathers, and feet. Solder in place.

Finish:
Clean with soap and water. ❖

Rondels Panel

You can use rondels as accents in the corners of windows or create a complete window filled with sparkling rondels as I've done here. They can be cut just like any other glass. You can also drill a small hole near the edge of a rondel, string it with monofilament line, and hang it in an empty window.

Size: 12-1/4" x 16-3/4"

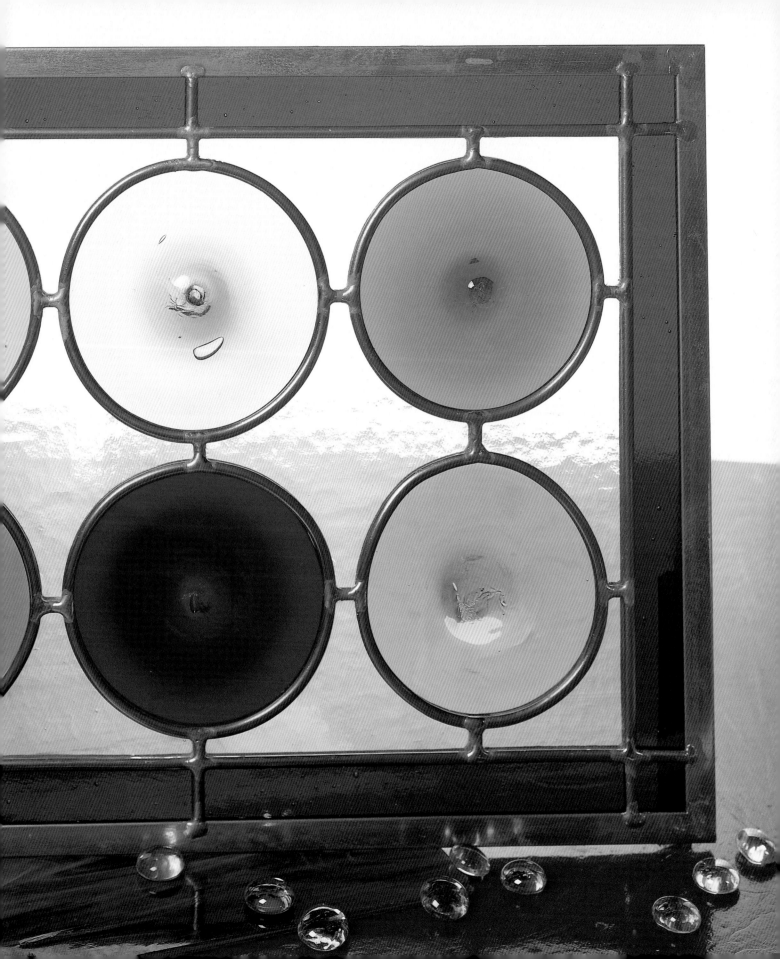

Supplies

Glass:
1 sq. ft. purple cathedral
2 sq. ft. light yellow cathedral
6 rondels, 4" diameter

Came:
3 6-ft. strips of 3/16" H lead
1 6-ft. strip of 3/8" U zinc

Tools:
Cementing supplies, see page 53
Basic Tools & Supplies as listed
China marker

Step-by-Step

Create Your Pattern:

As rondels are all handmade, their size and shape will vary. In order to properly cut the pieces for the panel that will fit around the rondels, you need to create a pattern that accommodates the particular rondels you will use.

1. On pattern paper, draw the outside lines of the panel, using the measurements provided.
2. Draw the 1" border.
3. Divide the inner section into equal-size squares, creating a grid.
4. Arrange the rondels inside the grid as you want them to be placed (a light box is helpful for this). Trace their shapes on your grid.
5. Label the rondels (you can use a china marker) and the pattern.

Prepare & Cut Glass:

1. Make two copies of the pattern. Number and mark the grain line on each piece of the background and border. Using pattern shears, cut out design from one copy. Trim the outer edges of the other copy of the pattern.
2. Adhere pattern pieces to the glass. Cut out each piece.
3. Use grozing pliers to remove any chips or protrusions on the glass pieces. Smooth the edges with a grinder or carborundum stone as needed to fit the pattern.
4. Stretch the lead came.

Lead Up & Solder:

1. On your work board, tape or pin the second copy of the pattern. Lay out the cut pieces of glass on the work board.
2. Lead up the panel, working from one corner, placing a piece of lead, a piece of glass, and so on, until all pieces are in place. Use the grinder to smooth edges of the glass and make adjustments. Each piece must fit the pattern lines.
3. Solder the joints on the top.
4. Turn project over and solder the joints on the back. *Note:* Because rondels are handmade, they have raised centers on them caused by the blowpipe. When you turn the panel over to solder the back, place padding under the panel so it will lay flat and the rondels won't get scratched. Do the same thing when you cement the panel.

Finish:

1. Cement and clean the panel. See note with step 4, above.
2. Drill holes for hooks or install in window or door. ❖

Rose Window pattern
Enlarge to 250% for actual size

Instructions on page 114

Rose Window Panel

Pale pink opalescent glass forms the background of this graceful window with vintage appeal.

Size: 18" x 23"

Supplies

Glass:
3 sq. ft. pale pink opalescent
1 sq. ft. of three different shades of green
1 sq. ft. deep pink
Light pink, 6" x 6"

Came:
5 6-ft. strips of 3/16" H lead
3 6-ft. strips of 1/8" H lead
2 6-ft. strips of 3/8" lead (for perimeter)

Other Supplies:
Black patina
Cementing supplies, see page 53

Tools:
Basic Tools & Supplies as listed

Step-by-Step

Prepare & Cut Glass:
1. Make two copies of the pattern. Number and mark the grain line on each piece. Using pattern shears, cut out design from one copy. Trim the outer edges of the other copy of the pattern.
2. Adhere pattern pieces to the glass. Cut out each piece.
3. Use grozing pliers to remove any chips or protrusions on the glass pieces. Smooth the edges with a grinder or carborundum stone as needed to fit the pattern.
4. Stretch the lead came.

Lead Up & Solder:
1. On your work board, tape or pin the second copy of the pattern. Lay out the cut pieces of glass on the work board.
2. Lead up the panel, working from one corner, placing a piece of lead, a piece of glass, and so on, until all pieces are in place. Use the grinder to smooth edges of the glass and make adjustments. Each piece must fit the pattern lines.
3. Solder the joints on the top.
4. Turn project over and solder the joints on the back.

Finish:
Cement and clean the panel. ❖

Tree House Birdhouse

This birdhouse is designed for decorative use only. It can be used outdoors or indoors, but it's not bird-friendly.

Supplies

Glass:
Brown opalescent, 16" x 6" and 6" x 6"
Green opalescent, 10" x 6"
Assorted glass beads

Came:
1 6-ft. strip of 3/16 H lead
2 6-ft. strips of 1/8" U lead

Other Supplies:
7/32" copper foil tape
1-1/2" brass vase cap
12 gauge copper wire
Silver paint pen
2 lb. empty coffee can

Tools:
Basic Tools & Supplies as listed
Needlenose pliers

Step-by-Step

Prepare & Cut Glass:

1. Make two copies of the pattern. Number and mark the grain line on each piece. Using pattern shears, cut out design from one copy. Trim the outer edges of the other copy of the pattern.
2. Adhere pattern pieces to the glass. Cut out each piece.
3. Use grozing pliers to remove any chips or protrusions on the glass pieces. Smooth the edges with a grinder or carborundum stone as needed to fit the pattern.
4. Stretch the lead came.

Assemble the Walls:

1. Apply copper foil tape around the edges of the birdhouse hole. Press foil tightly to the glass edge.
2. Place the second copy of the pattern on your work board. Trim off the excess paper along the left-hand side and bottom of the pattern. Slide the pattern into the right angle of your work board. Tape in place.
3. Place a 17" piece of U-shaped came along the bottom edge of the pattern against the work board. Place a 6" piece of H-shaped came along the left side of the pattern against the work board.
4. Fit the first piece of glass into the U channel. Put a 6" strip of H-shaped came on the right edge of this piece of glass. Insert the second piece of glass in the other side of the H channel. Continue building the walls of the birdhouse until all eight pieces are leaded

continued on page 118

Fig. 1 - Assembling the Walls
Back side of glass should be up; use tape to secure.

continued from page 116

up. Do not put a piece of lead along the edge of the last glass piece.

5. Cap off the walls by running a 16" U-shaped piece of came along the top edge of the eight pieces of glass.

6. Lightly tack solder the lead joints together. Use masking tape to support the glass walls. See Fig. 1.

7. Gently lift up the sides of the walls as one unit and shape into an octagon. Take your time and help form the shape with your hands. When the two outside edges come together, slip the glass edge in the channel of the H-shaped came to complete the octagon. Tack solder the joint where the two end pieces meet.

8. Stand the walls on a piece of pattern paper. Using a pencil, trace around the inside of the walls to make a pattern for the bottom of the tree house.

9. Cut out the pattern with pattern shears and adhere it to a piece of brown glass. Cut out the piece.

10. Test fit the glass in the bottom of the tree house. Remember to allow space for the lead came that will be wrapped around it.

11. Wrap the bottom piece in U-shaped lead came. Solder the joint where the two ends meet.

12. Slip the bottom piece inside the tree house and solder in place.

13. Solder the inside joints along the walls and reinforce any joints that may need more solder.

14. Apply an even coat of solder on the copper foil around the edge of the birdhouse opening.

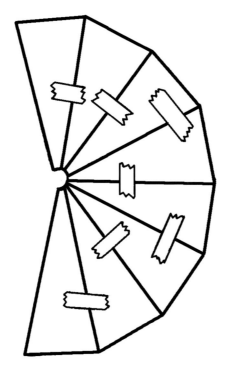

Fig. 2 - Assembling the Roof

Assemble & Attach the Roof:

1. Wrap all eight pieces of glass in U-shaped came, starting and stopping at the top of each piece. Secure each lead joint with solder.

2. Lay out the glass pieces, wrong side up, as shown in Fig. 2. Use masking tape to secure pieces in place, but **do not** solder.

3. Gently lift the ends of the roof sides up and shape all eight sides into a tent shape to form the roof. When you have the correct shape, solder the edges of the roof together. Secure the top and bottom edges with additional solder. Remove the tape from inside the roof.

4. Place the roof on the top of the walls. When it's on straight, secure with masking tape.

5. Turn the tree house upside down. Solder the roof to the sides from underneath the roof. Use an empty coffee can to support the tree house while you solder.

Finish:

1. Solder a 10-ft. piece of wire to the top of the birdhouse. Slip onto the wire the decorative vase cap and beads. Form a loop above the beads and twist the end of the wire to form a secure hook for hanging.

2. Use a paint pen to color the vase cap to match the lead came.

3. Clean project well with soap and water. ❖

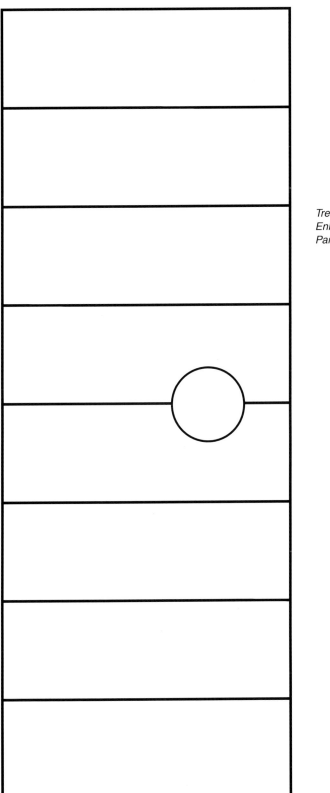

Tree House - walls
Enlarge to 195%
Panels measure 6" x 2"

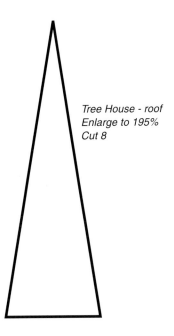

Tree House - roof
Enlarge to 195%
Cut 8

Forest Scene Fireplace Screen

This stained glass forest design is attached to a simple black wire fireplace screen (the kind you can buy at hardware and home improvement stores) with pieces of copper wire that are soldered to the back side of the lead came and threaded through the screen wire.

Use caution when using the screen—remember a roaring fire can get really hot and could overheat or crack the glass. Take care not to burn yourself or crack the glass from too much heat.

Supplies

Glass:
1 sq. ft. light brown (for large trees)
1 sq. ft. dark brown (for small trees)
1 sq. ft. rusty orange (for hill)
4 sq. ft. of four different greens (for meadow and trees)
1 sq. ft. blue ripple (for river)
1 sq. ft. green with purple (for hills)
1 sq. ft. yellow with white (for hills)
1 sq. ft. purple (for hills)

Came:
7 6-ft. strips of 1/8 H lead
1 6-ft. strip of 1/8" U zinc

Other Supplies:
12 gauge copper wire
Black wire fireplace screen
Cementing supplies, see page 53

Tools:
Basic Tools & Supplies as listed
Needlenose pliers
Came notcher

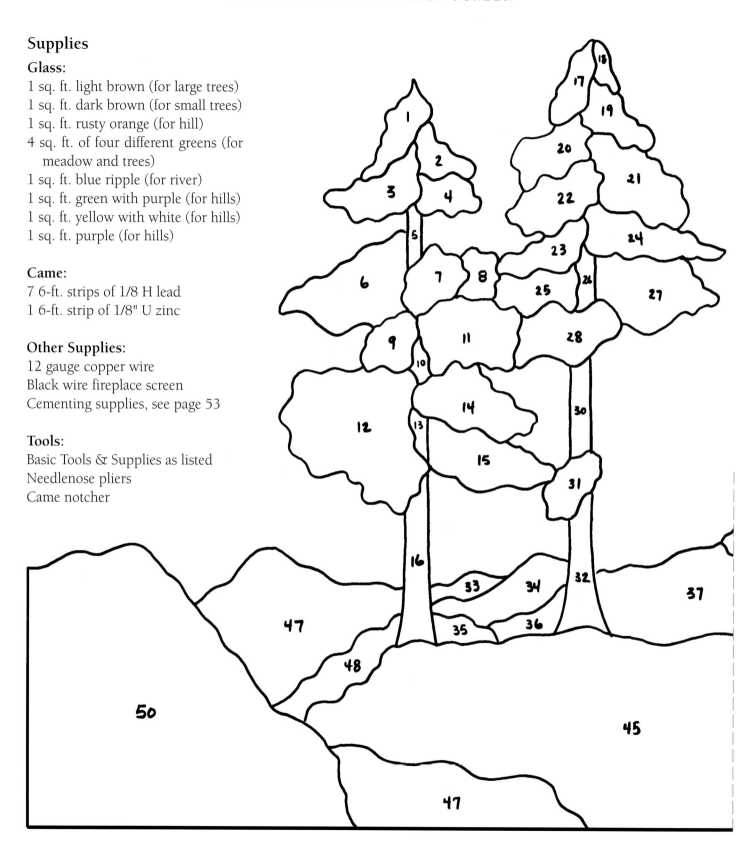

Step-by-Step

Prepare & Cut Glass:

1. Make two copies of the pattern. Number and mark the grain line on each piece. Using pattern shears and scissors, cut out design from one copy. Trim the outer edges of the other copy of the pattern.
2. Adhere pattern pieces to the glass. Cut out each piece.
3. Use grozing pliers to remove any chips or protrusions on the glass pieces. Smooth the edges with a grinder or carborundum stone as needed to fit the pattern.
4. Stretch the lead came.

Lead Up & Solder:

1. On your work board, tape or pin the second copy of the pattern. Lay out the cut pieces of glass on the work board.
2. Lead up the panel, working from one corner, placing a piece of lead, a piece of glass, and so on, until all pieces are in place. Use the U-shaped zinc came on the bottom and sides. Use the grinder to smooth edges of the glass and make adjustments. Each piece must fit the pattern lines.
3. Solder the joints on the top.
4. Turn project over and solder the joints on the back.

Finish:

1. Cement and clean the panel.
2. Cut ten 3" pieces of copper wire. Bend in half. On the back of the panel, solder the pieces of copper wire, selecting places that will best support the panel when it is attached to the screen.
3. Clean the back of the panel around the places where you've soldered.
4. Attach the panel to the screen. *Tips:* Use a helper and take the time to be sure your panel is well-supported and securely attached to the screen. ❖

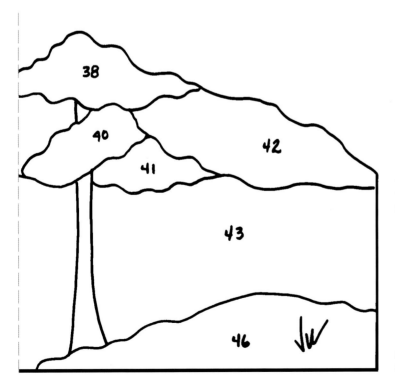

Since this pattern is a little more complicated, we have numbered the pieces to help you with assembly.

Forest Scene Fireplace Screen pattern
Enlarge to 215% for actual size

Brass Came
Bathroom Window

Stained glass and brass are the perfect solutions for bathroom windows. They are not affected by moisture and can provide as much or as little visibility as you need. The textured clear glass and bevels used in this window provide privacy and maximum light.

I used a bevel cluster for this project, but you could substitute textured or colored art glass. You'll find bevel clusters at your local stained glass shop or on the Internet.

Size: 15-1/2" x 23-1/2"

Supplies

Glass:
2 bevel clusters
3 sq. ft. clear textured iridized

Came:
3 6-ft. strips of 3/16" H brass
2 6-ft. strips of 1/8" U brass

Other Supplies:
Gold paint pen
Cementing supplies, see page 53

Tools:
Basic Tools & Supplies as listed
Came bender
Hacksaw *or* power came saw

Step-by-Step

Prepare & Cut Glass:
1. Make two copies of the pattern. Number and mark the grain line on each piece. Using pattern shears, cut out design from one copy. Trim the outer edges of the other copy of the pattern.
2. Adhere pattern pieces to the glass. Cut out each piece.
3. Use grozing pliers to remove any chips or protrusions from the pieces you cut. Smooth the edges with a grinder or carborundum stone as needed to fit the pattern.

Lead Up & Solder:
Brass came panels are built just like leaded ones. Use a hacksaw or power came saw to cut the brass came to size.
1. On your work board, tape or pin the second copy of the pattern. Lay out the cut pieces of glass on the work board.
2. Lead up the panel, working from one corner, placing a piece of came, a piece of glass, and so on, until all pieces are in place. Use the grinder to smooth edges of the glass and make adjustments. Each piece must fit the pattern lines.
3. Solder the joints on the top.
4. Turn project over and solder the joints on the back.

Finish:
1. Cement and clean the panel.
2. Use a gold paint pen to color the solder joints to match the brass came.
3. Install the panel in the window frame. ❖

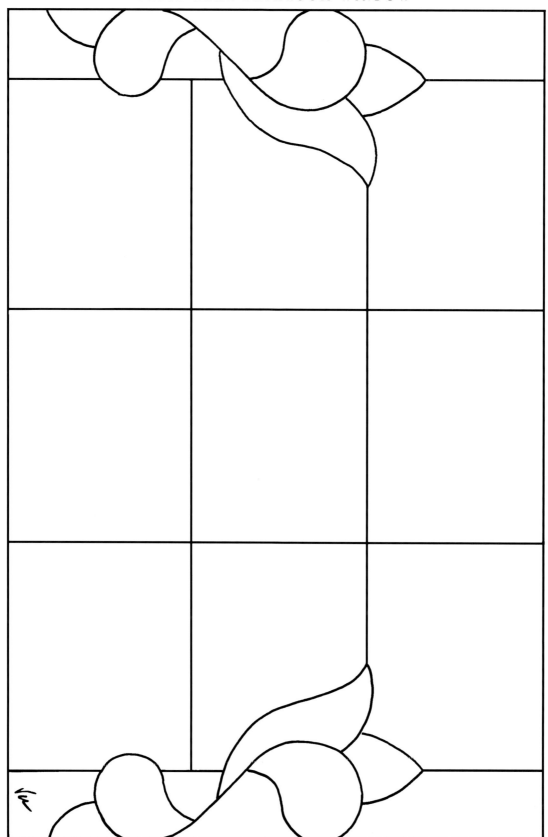

*Brass Came
Bathroom
Window
pattern*

*Enlarge to
267% for
actual size*

UP ▲

Metric Conversion Chart

Inches to Millimeters and Centimeters

Inches	MM	CM
1/8	3	.3
1/4	6	.6
3/8	10	1.0
1/2	13	1.3
5/8	16	1.6
3/4	19	1.9
7/8	22	2.2
1	25	2.5
1-1/4	32	3.2
1-1/2	38	3.8
1-3/4	44	4.4
2	51	5.1
3	76	7.6
4	102	10.2
5	127	12.7
6	152	15.2
7	178	17.8
8	203	20.3
9	229	22.9
10	254	25.4
11	279	27.9
12	305	30.5

Yards to Meters

Yards	Meters
1/8	.11
1/4	.23
3/8	.34
1/2	.46
5/8	.57
3/4	.69
7/8	.80
1	.91
2	1.83
3	2.74
4	3.66
5	4.57
6	5.49
7	6.40
8	7.32
9	8.23
10	9.14

Index